TalkforReading™

CREATING CURIOUS READERS

Talk for Writing
PO Box 286
HOLMFIRTH
HD9 9FF

Contact Nick Batty at orders@talk4writing.com
07514034010
www.talk4writing.com

First published, 2024

Copyright © Pie Corbett and Jamie Thomas

All rights reserved. The handouts referenced in this book may be printed to support in-school training only, but they remain the intellectual property of Pie Corbett and Jamie Thomas and are subject to copyright. It is forbidden to use the handouts for commercial gain, place them on the internet or share them with other schools or institutions. Except for the handouts on the Talk for Writing website and the use of brief extracts from the book for review purposes, no part of this publication may be reproduced or transmitted in any form or by any means, electronic or mechanical, including photocopy, recording, or any information and retrieval system, without permission in writing from the publisher (Talk for Writing) or a license from the Copyright Licensing Agency Ltd, Barnards Inn, 86 Fetter Lane, London EC4A 1EN (www.cla.co.uk).

ISBN: 978-1-9998942-8-3

British Library Cataloguing in Publication Data
A catalogue record of this book is available from the British Library.

- Editing, cover design, book layout and typesetting by Polly Barnett polly@pogolearning.com
- Film clips produced by imgfactory.co.uk
- Film icon designed by jonralphs.com
- Photographs: Julia Strong and Talk for Writing Training Schools

This book can only be ordered from www.talkforwritingshop.com

Creating Curious Readers:

Developing comprehension in primary schools

Pie Corbett and Jamie Thomas

Dedication

This book is dedicated to all the teachers and Talk for Writing schools and trainers who have helped develop Talk for Reading across the years. In particular, we would like to thank the teachers and schools who have contributed to this book. A special mention goes to Talk for Writing trainers Dean Thompson, Jane Ralphs and Julia Strong. Thanks to Mandy Nayton, CEO of DSF Literacy and Clinical Services and President of AUSPELD, for guidance and input on the teaching of phonics and the science of reading. Thanks also go to Bob Eaglestone, British literary critic and theorist and Professor of Contemporary Literature and Thought at Royal Holloway, University of London for many hours of conversation that helped shape ideas about dialogic comprehension and literary concepts.

To see the process in action and for information about training, please visit https://www.talk4writing.com/trainers/.

Pie Corbett and Jamie Thomas

Contents

All online handouts referenced throughout the book are available from www.talk4writing.com/cr using code 4891.

Video clips

The 20 video clips to support this book are available online. Go to www.talk4writing.com/cr and use code 4891 to access them.

The Introduction Phase

Video clip 1. Pie modelling and teaching prediction in Year 1 at Watermoor C of E Primary School, Cirencester.

Video clip 2. Jamie modelling explicit vocabulary teaching and gathering initial responses in Year 2 with *Kassim and the Greedy Dragon* at Warren Road Primary School, Orpington.

Video clip 3. Year 1 children demonstrating understanding of the vocabulary in *The Day the Crayons Quit* through action and expression at Warren Road Primary School, Orpington.

Video clip 4. Tracey Adams teaching vocabulary in Year 6 at St Matthew's C of E Primary School, Birmingham.

The Investigation Phase

Video clip 5. Pie demonstrating oral comprehension in Year 6 using *Voices in the Park* (part 1) at Knowle Park Primary School, Bristol.

Video clip 6. Pie demonstrating oral comprehension in Year 6 using *Voices in the Park* (part 2) at Knowle Park Primary School, Bristol.

Video clip 7. Jamie demonstrating oral comprehension in Year 2, using *Hansel and Gretel* at Warren Road Primary School, Orpington.

Video clip 8. Jamie investigating the prologue of *The Snow Walker's Son* in Year 6 at Warren Road Primary School, Orpington.

Video clip 9. Pie demonstrating bit-by-bit reading in Year 2 at The John Moore Primary School, Tewkesbury.

Video clip 10. Pie using dialogic techniques in Year 4 with *Elf Road* at Knowle Park Primary School, Bristol.

Video clip 11. Tracey Adams using a challenging non-fiction text on heroism in Year 6 at St Matthew's C of E Primary School, Birmingham.

Video clip 12. Dean Thompson reading a text bit-by-bit and co-constructing a toolkit with Year 4 children about the effect of authorial intent at Warren Road Primary School, Orpington.

Video clip 13. Tracey Adams teaching Year 6 children to summarise as part of a guided reading session at St Matthew's C of E Primary School, Birmingham.

Video clip 14. Jamie demonstrating the teaching of expression and intonation in Year 2 using *Hansel and Gretel* at Warren Road Primary School, Orpington.

Video clip 15. The power of performance – *Charge of the Light Brigade* at Selby Community Primary School, Selby.

The Independent Understanding Phase

Video clip 16. Pie modelling how to write a summary in response to *Cogheart* with a Year 4 class at The John Moore Primary School in Tewkesbury.

Video clip 17. A Year 5 child demonstrating understanding of *The Arrival* at Warren Road Primary School, Orpington.

Video clip 18. A Year 2 child demonstrating writing and performing in the style of Harold Monro in response to *Overheard on a Saltmarsh* at Warren Road Primary School, Orpington.

Video clip 19. A child in Reception independently re-telling *Overheard on a Saltmarsh* whilst playing in the provision at The John Moore Primary School, Tewkesbury.

Video clip 20. Three Year 2 children demonstrating their understanding of *Overheard on a Saltmarsh* through performance of the poem.

Foreword

Pie Corbett

The main approach to teaching comprehension in schools is based around getting children to answer set questions. It is usually based around isolated 'reading skills' such as vocabulary, summarising, inferring, imagining, locating information, identifying key points, etc. We believe that this has almost nothing to do with helping children to develop as readers. Such teaching is based on 'testing' – either you can answer the questions or not.

Talk for Reading is an approach that is based around dialogic reading. It aims to develop children's confidence as critical, appreciative and deep readers. At its core, a dialogic approach relies on the three-way relationship that lies at the heart of storytelling: the relationship between the teller, the listener and the story. In the classroom, this relationship is between the teacher, the child and the text.

Dialogic teachers introduce children to the chosen text as a rich experience – something to be imagined, inhabited and enjoyed. Our role is to help them form a personal connection with the text, making links with their own lives and reading world. *How does a text relate to our experiences, thoughts and feelings? In what ways does it matter to us? Does this text hold a special meaning for us (how I hated the rabbits in 'Watership Down', but sobbed when Aslan died)?* In this way, relationships are formed that can last a lifetime between texts and readers.

Dialogic reading involves discussion focused around helping children grow a bond with the text through their curiosity as readers. It builds the desire to read, think and explore deeply what a text means to each of us. Our sharing of ideas, if we work well together, will grow everyone's understanding. Through discussion, we build and challenge thinking so that ideas grow collectively and individually between the children, and between each child and the text. The student is very literally learning how to enter a conversation with what they read.

The teacher's job is to orchestrate these discussions and responses around a text rich with possibilities to help children make a personal connection. The teacher needs to read it with an eye to what might be easily understood, what might provide a challenge, and where it might be necessary to pause and re-read. Meagre reading and scant attention to the text by the teacher will only lead to impoverished comprehension.

One key aspect of dialogic comprehension is that the attention shifts from the teacher as the main focus of a lesson onto the children's growing understanding of the text. This is not about the teacher as guardian of the sole interpretation that the children have to guess. The focus is almost exclusively on the children's thinking in relation to the text. As a teacher, you need to learn how to listen most attentively. It may not be necessary to say much, but considerable effort should be put into thinking about what the children are saying and how to manage the discussion. It involves thinking about:

- when to allow a child to run with an idea;
- how to pause for further thought or to allow others to challenge or explain;
- when to return to the text to dig deeper;
- when to focus children on an aspect that might have been missed;
- how to grow confidence and deal sensitively with children as they wrangle critically with ideas;
- how to grow an atmosphere in which everyone is willing to participate, as well as being ready to change their thinking in the light of the conversation.

The job is ultimately to help the class create their own knowledge about the text, through rich discussion.

Of course, the joy of such teaching, in which the teacher appears to take a back seat and the children and text are placed more centrally, is that you usually learn from the discussion. New insights are often shared about texts as well as light thrown onto how the children think. This form of teaching does not come easily, as it puts aside the more familiar role of teacher as instructor. It has little to do with imparting knowledge, but everything to do with skilfully growing knowledge. It involves gaining understanding of the text and its layers of meaning, as well as learning about ourselves and our students. It is about growing the capacity for critical thinking.

In primary schools, teaching reading will involve some more direct approaches for aspects such as background knowledge, vocabulary and how to read non-fiction strategically. Dialogic teaching is a different – potentially more real and profound – kind of expertise for teachers to add to their repertoire. It dissolves the usual expert/novice distinction. In this approach, we recognise that the reader, the student, is the expert on their own feelings and how a text relates to their life and reading experience. The teacher's role is to pay very careful attention to this, learning more about how students think as readers as they orchestrate discussions. It is an approach to reading comprehension that runs from Reception classes to Higher Education.

Inevitably, the question arises about how such an approach might serve children in exam or test situations. In schools where dialogic teaching is one of a range of strategies used in different subjects, and students are given brief but relevant test preparation, we have found that becoming a dialogic reader helps them be better at exam-reading. They have strong self-images as readers, care about their reading and know how to read perceptively. It is worth adding that because a dialogic approach values what the children feel and think and how texts relate to them as people, they enjoy both their reading and discussions that probe and challenge. I remember an initial session on the opening of *Floodland* by Marcus Sedgwick taking about 50 minutes. I sent the Year 5 class outside to get some fresh air, but within a few minutes there were eager faces at the door, saying, *"we've thought of more we want to say"*. When we get it right, dialogic teaching grows the intellect, the capacity for critical thought, how to learn through rich discussions, and this hard work is a satisfying part of reading for pleasure.

The more such conversations are held, the more we hope to develop the habit of thoughtful reading so that readers are used to forming relationships with books, know how to pause, to wonder and re-read, considering the possibilities. Dialogic comprehension should lead to developing critical, appreciative readers who experience the joy of deep reading as a lifetime habit of mind.

This book digs deep into what effective Talk for Reading teachers and schools do in their work on reading. It explains the move from becoming familiar with a worthwhile and challenging text, digging deeper into the range of responses, possibilities and meanings, and finally demonstrating what has been learned.

Chapter 1: Overview of Talk for Reading

Pie Corbett

There are more conferences, training sessions, advisors and reading gurus than pebbles on a beach. There have been thousands of books written about teaching reading. Many are based on what research says, others are based on what someone has developed in their classroom or school and some are just ideas that someone has dreamed up and sound like a good prospect.

Talk for Reading is different because it is based on the work of effective schools where standards are regularly well above the national average, often despite the schools being in challenging areas. Unsurprisingly, much of the work is echoed in research. However, our approach is firmly rooted in the practicalities of what works, in a range of schools, from those serving some of the most challenging areas of the country through to the most privileged areas, from inner city to village school.

The drive to develop our work on reading was triggered by the English annual SATs papers in 2016, which were pitched at a higher standard than previously. Many schools that had, over the years, high attainment, found standards falling dramatically. However, some of the Talk for Writing training centres and other schools continued to attain at a high level. This encouraged us to think about what these schools were doing that made a difference. Together, we developed Talk for Reading.

To begin, Dean Thompson and I carried out a review of effective practice during 2016 and 2017, focusing on schools in deprived areas that maintained very high standards, despite the challenge of the new tests. We talked with and visited successful schools to find out what made the difference and drew upon current research. All the schools used a Talk for Writing approach. They also had many common strands in their approach to teaching reading. We worked with a group of schools over about four years to develop and refine the common strands that were related to success. This refinement of practice is constant and will continue as we discover more about developing children who are confident, critical and appreciative readers. There are a few overarching aspects of developing a successful school. Not surprisingly, the first is to do with very strong leadership.

In the successful schools, it was noticeable that the leadership team drove the reading programme. In our 2017 review, we wrote:

> ***a. Leaders know what is happening: there is an agreed and established reading curriculum associated with a pattern to teaching reading that is well supported with professional development and the impact is regularly monitored. The senior management team constantly check through the careful use of learning walks, regular observations, and pupil discussions as well as regular staff meetings. The curriculum is refined in the light of effectiveness.***
>
> ***b. The impact is carefully checked: a range of data and regular assessments, as well as knowing the children as readers, is all used to identify what is working and adaptations to the programme are swiftly made. Those who fall behind are rapidly identified and given extra practice rather than weaknesses being accepted or coming as a surprise at the end of a key stage. Assessment materials such as the York Assessment of Reading Comprehension (YARC) are used to pick up on issues such as weak decoding, poor vocabulary, or lack of fluency as well as comprehension issues.***
>
> ***c. Teaching is constantly updated and thoughtfully refined in the light of experience. They use SATs data (English national test results) to focus teaching, but are just as keen to monitor children's motivation. The school's programme is non-negotiable, vigorously led and supported by constant ongoing training. This is followed up with in-class support and coaching as well as monitoring.***
>
> ***d. Leaders keep in touch with current research and development; they are relentlessly curious about other effective schools, focused on discovering what makes effective teaching and learning and make regular visits to successful schools. Reading is central to the culture of the school and is directly led by the Head and senior staff.***

Getting maximum impact

When we began our review, it was obvious that there were four different ingredients that were common to all the schools:

- very strong leadership;
- effective teaching of early reading;
- commitment to reading for pleasure;
- a focus on teaching comprehension.

Dean Thompson, a Talk for Writing trainer, represented the core elements that all the maximum-impact schools shared through the Venn diagram below. **This helped clarify our understanding that any school has to develop these three core aspects of reading, each as strongly as the other.**

1. Reading culture
2. Learning to read
3. Learning to comprehend
    - The three phases of Talk for Reading

If one of these strands is weak, then the impact of the school's efforts will be lessened. All three strands are essential and must be well-developed so that they become part of the school's culture and not dependent on any one member of staff. Below is a brief overview of these three aspects.

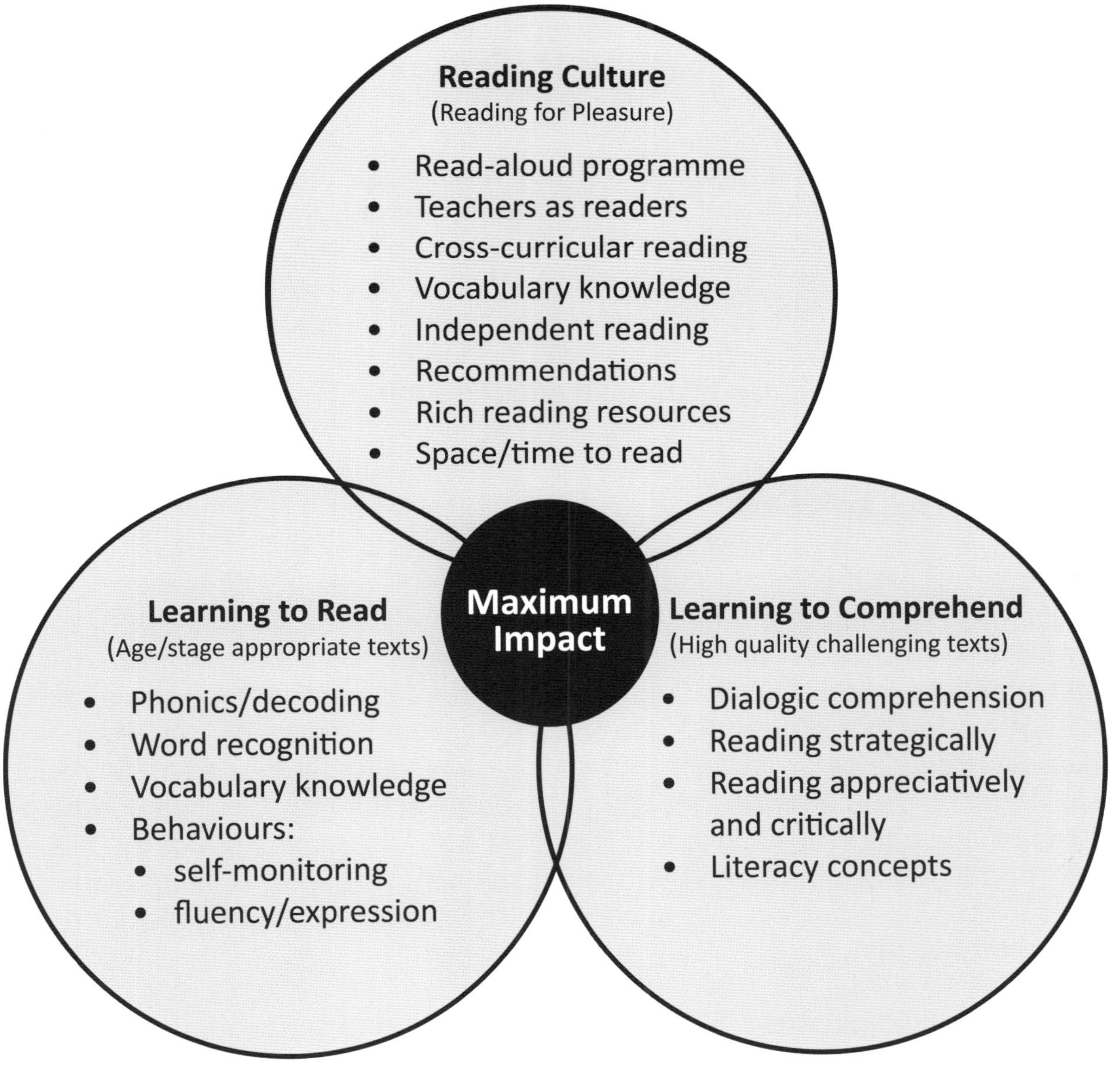

1. Reading culture

If children and teachers do not love reading, then children are unlikely to read enough to become fluent so that reading is automatic, effortless and a pleasure. To some extent, fluency is a matter of practice. Children need to clock up considerable reading mileage. To become readers, they need a large amount of being read to, reading together and reading independently. The cornerstone of growing *Reading for Pleasure* in a classroom and school stems from a combination of the teachers' passion for reading and sharing great books and authors. Where reading is not rated as a key pastime, teachers lack enthusiasm for, and knowledge of, literature.

The reading culture in a school has to be developed so that reading becomes central to the life of the school; that it matters in every class, to every teacher, every family and to every child. In successful schools, children love reading and avidly consume books. They are knowledgeable about authors, have met many, have been involved in Book Weeks and work with teachers who are passionate and knowledgeable about reading. The schools are well resourced with a wide variety of texts from comics to graphic novels to great novels, picture books, poetry and non-fiction.

A key starting point for developing a strong reading culture that several schools used is to survey children and staff. Through the survey, alongside discussions with classes and interviews with children, parents and staff, a picture can be built up of the current state of play. *Is it a school where children love reading? What do the children like to read? Are the resources matched to what they like reading? Can the provision be improved?* The survey then must lead to action and approaches for improvement built into the subject development plan.

2. Learning to read

Alongside a great reading culture, successful schools are very effective at teaching the foundation skills of reading. Children need to apply their increasing knowledge of phoneme-grapheme relationships to read and spell, gradually increasing their word recognition skills so that they can read and write effortlessly, automatically and at a reasonable rate. It is, as Mark Seidenberg suggests, as if they can *"read by sight"*. Ultimately, this means that as children develop fluency, they can focus on meaning rather than laboriously decoding and encoding each word. They shift from the mechanics of the task to comprehending and composition, alongside enjoying what is being read or created. If every word is a struggle, then there is little cognitive space for comprehension.

Daily time-tabled **phonics** teaching, applied into writing and reading is sacrosanct. Successful schools use a sound-to-print approach so that 'phonics for spelling' leads into success with early writing as well as strengthening decoding. They ensure that the ability to read a word and spell a word develops at a similar pace, with these two skills being taught as reversible processes (we blend to read and segment to spell). Considerable effort should be put into the teaching of phonics, in recognition of the central role it plays in the development of reading and spelling accuracy and fluency. To this extent, successful schools draw on the science of reading which shows that, for children to become skilled readers, phonic knowledge is a necessary, but not sufficient, underlying skill.

As children increase their knowledge of our complex written code and their reading and writing becomes increasingly automatic, more attention can be directed towards comprehension. The capacity to comprehend text is heavily dependent on working memory which, for children in the first few years of school, is very limited. As novice readers, most of their available working memory is being used to decode, rather than comprehend. This can also be described in terms of cognitive load, which essentially refers to the total amount of mental effort or energy being used in working memory. Skilled reading, and reading comprehension, in particular, is viewed as being cognitively very demanding.

Comprehension can be thought of as an active and dynamic **process** that we cannot see. It happens during reading, not after reading. The reader needs to bring information stored in their long-term memory system (including vocabulary, lexical and syntactic knowledge, topic-specific knowledge and personal experience) to the text they are reading. To comprehend text, readers must translate the language they are reading into a ‘picture’ of the content. This is sometimes referred to as a mental model, and includes both the linguistic information from the text and the reader’s own prior knowledge. Younger children find this process more challenging and benefit from pictures and additional scaffolding to help visualise the content or build an accurate mental model. If children (at any age) do not have sufficient background knowledge, including vocabulary, to actively engage in the text they are reading, then this should be provided prior to reading. This allows the child to both build a mental model, and monitor the text closely, as they read.

Comprehension monitoring is a strategy that can be modelled by the teacher and encouraged. Stopping at key points in the text, reflecting or ‘thinking aloud’ about unusual language, character choices or plot developments, helps children to do the same when they read. The use of graphic organisers, questions for discussion, summarising and learning about text structure are also useful comprehension building capacities. Ultimately, however, the most important strategies revolve around those that enable students to actively engage with the texts they read **as they read them**, such as vocabulary, text structure and topic-specific knowledge.

In the early stages of phonics instruction, to ensure that children are improving their language **comprehension** and broadening their understanding and vocabulary, daily sessions of shared reading focus on experiencing high quality picture books, early novels, oral storytelling, poetry and information. Initially, the teacher will be modelling different concepts of print as well as the basics of book-handling. The teacher takes full responsibility for reading, so that the children can focus on comprehension. As children become more proficient, they may be able to read along with the teacher. In some cases, they may know the books so well that they can recite sections. Although this is not reading as such, it is giving children access to the language and structure of written texts, which is very important for literacy development.

In the early stages of teaching reading, word reading and language comprehension are two strong threads, both equally important. Children are rigorously taught **phonics** and, alongside this, oral **comprehension** is also developed through the explicit teaching of vocabulary and the use of quality picture books, short novels, information texts and rhymes.

As the rate of reading increases, children become more able to think about what they are reading. This ability to read automatically and effortlessly, at a reasonable rate, with understanding, leads towards **fluency**: reading expressively with understanding. Fluency is a skill that needs developing and the push towards 'performance reading' (reading aloud with expression) demands that the young reader becomes increasingly used to tracking the meaning in order to perform with expression. This arises from modelling by the teacher, echoing well-read sentences and passages and developing the habit of reading accurately at the same time as giving meaning to the text. This takes **considerable reading practice** alongside increasing world and word knowledge. The more children read fluently, the more we are able to dig deeper into challenging, quality texts. We cannot emphasise enough that children of all ages benefit enormously from reading, ideally a considerable amount.

3. Learning to comprehend

Talk for Reading focuses on developing the comprehension strand, which sits within a strong reading culture, matched by effective teaching of reading, and underpinned by successful leadership. Talk for Reading is structured to help children learn to read critically, appreciatively and confidently. It aims to develop children into efficient, effective, thoughtful and strategic readers who can learn about life, discover information and deepen their thinking through considering other people's views and experiences with a critical mind. Our young readers should read **critically**, not accepting everything they read at surface value. They should read **appreciatively** so that they develop a taste for great literature, but can also enjoy a light read for what it is. Neither of these things happen if children are not confident in their ability to read **thoughtfully** and **strategically**, knowing that the effort to tackle demanding texts is worthwhile.

Many of us love reading as escapism, leaving behind the mundane world and entering a secondary space where we become someone else in a different world. The gift of reading means that we can enjoy and perhaps challenge the finest words and thoughts and ideas that mankind has to offer. Talk for Reading develops the habit of reading and thinking deeply, developing a critical and appreciative stance. Deep and avid readers participate in the reading conversation that has lasted a thousand years, allowing us to enter the minds and inner worlds of those long dead, the greatest thinkers and the most beautiful of worlds. It allows children to reflect upon themselves and their lives and probably enhances their ability to comprehend their own existence.

A key aspect of developing reading is through daily teaching of vocabulary and knowledge. This must be both within English sessions and also across the curriculum. We noticed that successful schools teach the language of different subjects and have higher expectations than most schools. It is not uncommon to see children in a science lesson being taught to say, *"we are investigating"*, *"my prediction"* or *"to create a fair test"*, in Year 1. Of course, a rich and thought-provoking curriculum will also help deepen children's comprehension as their world knowledge increases.

The approach of Talk for Reading, like Talk for Writing, uses the gradual-release-of-responsibility model, shifting children from dependence towards independence. Through the exploration of a challenging text, children gather their initial responses before deepening their understanding of the core themes that lie at its heart. As part of this exploration, they also consider how the text works and how it has been created, as well as making links with other areas of study, other texts and life itself.

During a unit, not only do the children read, respond and deepen understanding of a multi-layered text, but also draw on the text by writing in the same style. Alternatively, they could use the same writing idea, innovate on the text or write critically about their understanding. A unit may take three weeks, but work on a single haiku may take one session. Talk for Reading is a set of principles and practices that are effective, but they have to be used thoughtfully by teachers to meet the demands of the text, the needs of the children and any relevant national curriculum requirements.

The three phases of Talk for Reading

Talk for Reading is planned around the gradual release of responsibility model. It has three phases that build to the final phase of children being able to comprehend the text or apply the learning independently:

a. The Introduction Phase
b. The Investigation Phase
c. The Independent Understanding Phase

The Talk for Reading teaching sequence

The Introduction Phase

Achieve basic understanding:

Before reading

- hook;
- context;
- activate prior knowledge.

While reading

- teacher models reading with fluency;
- prediction;
- initial responses;
- re-reading;
- initial vocabulary;
- literal retrieval;
- establish focus.

The Investigation Phase

Deepen understanding of the focus through:

- oral comprehension;
- strategic reading;
- response activities;
- exploring structure and effect;
- summarising;
- evaluating;
- reading fluently.

The Independent Understanding Phase

Demonstrate understanding through either:

- talking or writing as a reader about the core text; or
- identifying the key focus in another text and responding; or
- applying what they have learned in their own writing.

By the end of the **Introduction Phase**, the children have a basic understanding of the text. It has been re-read several times, initial responses logged and core vocabulary considered. The teacher models fluent reading. Understanding may be at a basic level, though deeper thinking may have begun.

The **Investigation Phase** is where the class begin to 'dig deep' into the focus for the unit, exploring the text's core purpose. They may well have to use a strategic approach to clarify meaning. Response activities, such as drama or writing in role as a character, may be used to build a close relationship between the reader and the text. The phase ends with summarising the main ideas, information, viewpoints, events or themes and evaluation. At this point, the children can all read the text confidently and fluently with understanding.

In the final **Independent Understanding Phase**, children will demonstrate understanding independently. This may be through talking or writing about the text in a discursive style, answering in-depth questions about the text, applying what they have learned to new texts, or writing something similar (drawing on the same style and structure).

These three phases are explained in detail in **Chapters 3-5**. Choosing which texts to use is a key focus of **Chapter 2: Preparing to teach a reading unit**. Talk for Reading is not about teaching 'exam/test reading', isolated 'skills' or 'strategies'. It is about developing children's ability to read strategically in order to gain the core purpose from a challenging, quality text. Our focus is on the active engagement of the reader during reading so that links can be made and connections developed and refined in the light of new information, gradually building a mental model of the text. Another key aspect of Talk for Reading is that children are increasingly developing an understanding of the core literary concepts such as viewpoint, symbolism or characterisation. Whilst a unit on *Voices in the Park* by Anthony Browne will help the children enjoy the whole book, it will also help them develop an understanding of 'viewpoint' – of the narrator, the reader and the various characters. These understandings will carry over into enriching their reading of other texts.

Chapter 2: Preparing to teach a reading unit

Pie Corbett

Talk for Reading is not a mechanistic routine or procedure that always follows exactly the same pattern. As a teacher, you need to select a worthwhile text and then decide how it will be taught to help children get the most out it so that by the end of the unit, children have understood, enjoyed and learned from the text – as well as deepening their understanding of key literary concepts. It is important to take time to consider how best to achieve a well-considered sequence of learning that will steadily deepen understanding of a text, rather than the teaching becoming a dull, mechanistic routine.

The aim of Talk for Reading is to:

- help children to appreciate and enjoy the whole text;
- focus and build the reader's response, deepening understanding;
- develop effective, critical and appreciative readers;
- develop skilful readers who read avidly, strategically and with curiosity;
- develop understanding of key literary concepts.

Our goal is to help children understand and appreciate the content of the text, not to practise a particular reading skill. This chapter is organised into the following sections:

1. Selecting quality, challenging texts
    - Ensuring a balanced programme of text types
2. Deciding what the text is about
    - Linking to first-hand experience
3. Choosing the comprehension focus
    - The initial brainstorm around literary concepts
    - The unit synopsis
    - Positive reading habits
4. Preparing for the three phases of Talk for Reading
    - The Introduction Phase
    - The Investigation Phase
    - The Independent Understanding Phase
5. Teaching the text
    - Initial vocabulary
    - Planning discussion points and key questions
6. Assessing and supporting individual readers who struggle

1. Selecting quality, challenging texts

Unsurprisingly, the first thing to do is to carefully select a short text to focus on, that is rich with possibility, and decide which aspects of teaching reading it demands. If a text is too easy, then not much will be learned. It should be pitched well above the independent reading level of the whole class because it means that:

- strategic reading has to be used;
- teaching can take place;
- children learn more.

Ideally your chosen text should fit into an overall 'reading curriculum' that identifies which novels, short stories, extracts, poems and non-fiction texts are to be studied. Each year group should cover a range of non-fiction, poetry and stories – and the selection should be based on what is usually referred to as 'quality literature', in its broadest sense. By 'literature' we mean the full range of written texts (which can also include graphic texts and film). By quality, we mean texts that:

- present new ideas, introduce enduring philosophical and ethical viewpoints and challenge stereotypes;
- contain the finest words and thoughts expressed;
- will stay with the reader forever as part of their inner life;
- touch on and illuminate eternal truths about the human condition;
- introduce and explore a range of information, new ideas and challenging viewpoints so that the reader understands themselves, others and our world better;
- are relevant to children's lives and their understanding of our times or current affairs and the rich diversity of life;
- provide a rich variety of language, image and emotion.

There are various reasons for mapping this across a school. Firstly, it means that multi-copies of core texts can be purchased. You also become familiar with the texts over time, gaining expertise about the depth of their content. This will enable teaching plans to be developed so that literary notions are cumulatively built on and themes revisited, deepening children's ability to read critically. Our successful schools have taken several years to develop their curriculum and constantly tweak it in the light of its impact, continually questioning whether it works.

At Yew Tree Community Primary School in Birmingham, the staff have been working on their reading curriculum for a number of years and are still refining it. The texts studied may be short stories, poems, picture books, short non-fiction texts or extracts from great novels (though if using extracts from novels, it is important to ultimately read the whole book). Developing a programme over an extended period of time can be achieved through working with teachers, as a school management team and by using one of our consultants. We believe that it is important to customise the programme to the community and setting.

Core texts studied in English are often supported by a cluster of other texts to deepen children's comprehension and engagement. For example, children's understanding of *Letters from a Lighthouse* by Emma Carroll, is deepened if they know some background information about evacuees to help 'set the scene'. However, choosing texts to go together on the basis of subject matter can miss the point. For instance, *The Three Little Pigs* is not necessarily enhanced by reading about pigs! This is because the story is not actually about pigs – it could have been about goats or sheep or mice. The story's heart is about becoming independent, doing things well and defeating the monster through collective endeavour!

It is often more effective to link texts that explore the same theme. I once saw a session in which Anthony Browne's *Voices in the Park* began with an introduction about gorillas! It might be better to tune into the theme of the story by thinking about viewpoints, relationships, alienation and hope through texts like, *I'll take you to Mrs Cole!* by Nigel Gray and *The True Story of the 3 Little Pigs* by Jon Scieszka.

A fiction example (using a novel)

When using novels, you may wish to choose extracts that explore specific focuses. For example, if you were teaching a Year 4 class and had chosen *Varjak Paw* by S. F. Said as your novel, then you could select one or two short passages (one or two sides of A4) as the focus for your reading unit to answer questions like these.

- *How does S. F. Said introduce conflict in the first chapter of* ***Varjak Paw****?*
- *In Chapter 34, does S. F. Said resolve the conflicts?*

The comprehension focus can then be extended and embedded when reading the whole novel, which is best read as part of a daily read-aloud programme so that children can experience and discuss the text together.

Meanwhile, in your writing unit, you might be using the short story *Zelda Claw* which was written to accompany the novel, but uses a simpler structure and language to provide a challenging, yet realistic writing model for the class. This is an important point to note: sourcing your model text for writing from novels is often not a good idea as children are not writing novels. However, using extracts from novels to identify authorial technique and purpose, will no doubt enrich the writing.

A non-fiction example (using a discussion text)

In St Matthew's C of E Primary School in Birmingham, we filmed Tracey Adams, the Year 6 teacher, working on a discussion text comparing Carlyle's view on heroism using a short extract from *On Heroes, Hero-Worship, and the Heroic in History* with a short extract from the philosopher Nietzsche (**see video clip 11**). The idea of the text choice was so that it would help children discuss heroism in their core Talk for Writing story, *Beowulf*. Here is an extract of the discussion text they looked at:

"Friedrich Nietzsche's theory of the ubermensch (sometimes translated as 'superman') speaks to this concept of going beyond human ability. Nietzsche, a 19th century German philosopher wrote in 'Thus Spoke Zarathustra' (1883) that in the modern world God, or the concept of God, had ceased to give life meaning. This void, he wrote, could be filled by the ubermensch, a superior, transcendent human being who would give new meaning to life."

Ensuring a balanced programme of text types

Initial planning should begin by looking across a term and ensuring that there is a balance of fiction, non-fiction and poetry – while considering their role within the overall curriculum. It is essential that schools do not over-complicate this. When deciding which texts to include, use the questions below to help guide you.

- *Will this text interest the children?*
- *Does it add something new to their knowledge?*
- *Is it sufficiently challenging so that children will have to read strategically?*
- *Is there something about the text that requires deep thinking?*
- *Is it just one text or can we cluster a few texts together that inform each other, e.g. a poem, picture book and short story?*
- *Have we covered a variety and diversity of texts over the year?*

Text selection is so important that all those responsible for reading across the school should be involved. It's also important to ensure:

- that there is progression across each year;
- that there is progression from one year to the next;
- that the core aims and literary concepts are being cumulatively revisited and built upon;
- that there is evident impact of the school's programme on the children's enjoyment of reading, amount of independent reading and attainment.

2. Deciding what the text is about

The first thing to do with any text selected is to closely read and decide what the text is actually about. *What lies at the heart of this text?* To decide how to approach a text, you need to devote time to re-reading, annotating and thinking deeply about it.

It pays to base your annotations on simple question prompts.

- *What core vocabulary needs teaching?*
- *Is there any essential background knowledge to provide?***
- *Where are the 'pinch points' where comprehension might slip away?*
- *Where might children miss the significance of what is happening?*
- *How does the word-choice, grammar and structure affect the reader?*
- *What are the key themes/big ideas/pieces of information?*

**A word of warning about background knowledge. A good text should establish its context and be an enjoyable experience without too much fuss. A story can be killed by an excess of background information and tenuous links, so limit this to what is essential to deeper understanding. We don't have to travel to Narnia, look after a unicorn, or be flattened so thin so that we can be slipped under a door to understand the narrative of these stories. Likewise, we don't need to ride in a sky-ship to enjoy *Brightstorm*. A well-written text will build the story world that the reader needs. Do we have to know all there is about the First World War to have appreciated Sebastian Faulk's *Birdsong*?

Sometimes, a link made by theme can be helpful: Jill Paton Walsh's novel *Fireweed* is set in the Blitz but is actually about loneliness, survival, friendship and rejection. *Dogger* by Shirley Hughes is not about losing a fluffy toy but about sacrifice. The skilled teacher of reading finds the heart of the text. We have found that getting teachers to discuss this aspect of Talk for Reading is important as it isn't always easy to establish what lies at the core of a text.

Having said that, it is also rather obvious that if a child is reading a text about skateboarding and is familiar with the terminology and territory, then they are going to understand more. Prior knowledge will be most important when reading information about specific subjects such as basketball, nuclear physics or Henry VIII. In general, books about life – most novels and picture books – are more accessible as the reader already has sufficient life experience to make connections.

Linking to first-hand experience

The cunning teacher considers carefully the text and its place within the curriculum. For instance, if we used the wonderful book *Just Ducks* by Nicola Davies with a Reception class, then hatching ducklings and a trip to the park to see the ducks would set the scene very powerfully for a rich reading and will make understanding easier. I once saw a Reception teacher showing children ears of wheat and discussing the process of grinding wheat to make flour, before reading *The Little Red Hen*. After about 15 minutes, a little voice said, *"Can't we just have the story?"* The pre-teaching of her inner-city class fell on deaf ears! Perhaps the story would have sat better within the context of a farm visit, baking bread and a discussion about helping each other.

Ideally, experiences need to be first-hand and as rich as possible. I still recall Year 2 children doing a drama activity based on riding on a train into London with the teacher enthusiastically pointing out the dome of St Paul's and Nelson's Column. Part of the issue was that most of the class had never been on a train and didn't understand what she was referring to. They went along with it, but many had that rather baffled look on their faces that seemed to suggest, *"What is she on about?"* Of course, we can make connections between our own experience and new situations, but a walk in the park hardly prepares you for a story based on the Amazon Rainforest.

3. Choosing the comprehension focus

This requires careful consideration and can only be planned once you have established what is at the heart of the text. The aim is for children to understand the whole text and deepen understanding of any core literary concepts.

> Teaching literature, in its broadest sense, involves deepening the core aspects of literary study which are expressed as ***variations*** and ***combinations*** of the main literary concepts listed below.
>
> - Role of characters/issues/information (as applicable)
> - Role of setting/mood/tone (as applicable)
> - Structure of text – how the text works
> - Use of language, including figurative language
> - Perspective/viewpoints – writer/narrator/character/reader
> - Main themes/ideas/arguments
>
> When planning the unit of work, it is important that we consider how the literary concepts contribute to the purpose of the text.

The initial brainstorm around literacy concepts

When choosing which of the literary concepts contribute to the purpose of the text, look at each in turn and consider how it might be relevant. High quality, challenging texts will inevitably explore more than one concept. Decide which to delve into further across the unit of work in order to deepen understanding of the text. Below are a few prompts.

Role of characters/issues/information (as applicable)

- *How are the characters/issues/information presented?*
- *Are there issues around stereotyping or bias in the text?*
- *Are there significant relationships/themes/issues explored?*
- *What happens to the main characters? How does this change them and what is the impact?*
- *What are the characters' motivators and drivers?*
- *Which parts of the dialogue/action are significant?*
- *How are characters/issues/information seen by others in the text?*
- *How do we learn about the main characters?*
- *What are the key issues and counter points/arguments?*
- *Is the information or issues explored significant?*
- *How does the author feel about the characters, issues and information?*

Role of setting/mood/tone (as applicable)

- *How does the author use language to build a setting, create a mood or tone?*
- *What is the influence of the setting on the character or events?*
- *How does the author manipulate the reader through setting, tone or atmosphere created?*
- *Are the illustrations influential? Do they evoke emotion? What is the relationship between illustrations and graphics, and what is written?*
- *How does the setting make the reader feel – inviting/uninviting?*
- *How does the use of colour in the illustrations of the setting define or suggest the mood?*
- *How does the author use the senses to build imagery and atmosphere?*
- *How does the author use unfamiliarity in a setting to create intrigue (for the character and the reader)?*
- *Does the author use a 'zoom in focus' to provide intensity, detail or change viewpoint?*
- *How can the setting take on the role of a character in the story?*
- *What tone is used and how does this effect the reader, e.g. authoritative, formal, informal?*
- *In non-fiction, how does the author create a mood and to what effect?*

Structure of text – how the text works

- *How is the text structured/laid out?*
- *How does the author organise information?*
- *How does the structure help/hinder the reader?*
- *How do paragraphs build the text?*
- *Does the text explore different viewpoints and perspectives? If so, how is this organised and what is the impact on the meaning/reader?*
- *What is the effect of the text following a linear/non-linear pattern?*
- *What is the significance of the prologue/epilogue/flashbacks or forwards/pivotal moments/plot twists/cliff hanger/summary or conclusion?*
- *Where are there shifts/changes and key pivotal episodes?*
- *How are illustrations/graphics used to support the impact?*

Use of language, including figurative language

- *How do word choices and sentence patterns create effect?*
- *How does figurative language create emotions, images, symbols and ideas?*
- *How does the pattern or rhythm of the text support meaning?*
- *What is the effect of the balance between description, dialogue and action?*

Perspectives/viewpoints – author/narrator/character/reader

- *How does the author influence the text? Is their viewpoint clear, biased or impartial?*
- *Is there a difference between the viewpoint of the narrator and the characters in the story?*
- *Does the text explore more than one character viewpoint or perspective, or line of argument?*
- *Are the viewpoints complementary or contrasting?*
- *How might different readers interpret the text, e.g. girls, boys, adults, teachers, politicians, etc.?*
- *How does prior knowledge or experience alter our understanding or opinion of the text?*

Main themes/ideas/arguments

- *What are the key themes, ideas and arguments that lie at the heart of the text?*
- *How is the main theme/idea explored and developed?*

- *What are the counter points, alternative views or shades of meaning explored in the text?*
- *Are there any sub-plots that are influential?*

The initial brainstorming opens up the potential of the text. Having decided which concept/s will be the focus of the unit, it helps to draw up a brief unit synopsis. This is an overview of what the children might learn or have considered by the end of the unit.

The unit synopsis

The unit synopsis captures the overarching objectives for the unit – the core elements of reading that we hope the children will be able to demonstrate with increasing independence over time. It is important to note that these are not a checklist of skills. Instead, they link to the core literary concepts being explored and will focus on the transferable elements of learning. These will be central to assessing outcomes at the **Independent Understanding Phase** (see **Chapter 5**).

Here are some examples of unit synopses linked to character and setting.

By the end of the unit, children might be able to:

- talk about different characters and their personalities in a text;
- compare and contrast characters and justify their opinions by making reference to the text;
- talk about what motivates a character and how this may impact their behaviour.

By the end of the unit, children might be able to:

- discuss how the author creates suspense, referencing the role of the setting to enhance the atmosphere;
- discuss how characters can be used to build mystery;
- talk about the purpose of a prologue and explore the way the author starts the novel to hook the reader and provide foreshadowing.

Further examples of the initial brainstorming around literary concepts and the writing of unit synopses can be found in **Chapter 8**.

Positive reading habits

In addition to their comprehension of the text, children should also be shown how to develop positive reading habits (sometimes referred to as strategies), as set out on the next page.

- **Responding** – the habit of engaging with the text and relating it to their own experience. Talk for Reading is primarily about developing children's confidence in their own responses and then equipping them with the knowledge about literature and the language they need to engage in ongoing class discussions. If children are not in the habit of discussing and shaping their ideas, then they are more likely to find it hard to 'think' in their heads as they read.
- **Predicting** – the habit of wondering what might happen next. Being able to follow lines of thought and set up expectations that might be confirmed, refined or proven to be completely incorrect.
- **Clarifying** – the habit of tying the text together as the reading builds up and adapting ideas and scenes in the light of new information. Where meaning falls apart, knowing how to discriminate between small slippages that might not matter and big points where re-reading strategically might be needed.
- **Questioning** – the habit of wondering what will happen as well as being ready to critically think about the text.
  - *Does this ring true?*
  - *Do people really behave like that?*
  - *Isn't that out of character?*
  - *That's a weak argument.*
  - *This writer holds unacceptable views.*
- **Imagining** – the habit of responding to the imagery by visualising what is happening. Being able to emotionally engage with characters by making links to their own life and feelings to understand the text at a deeper level.
- **Noticing text structure and language** – knowing that the glossary might help define a new term; using chapter headings, subheadings and an index; referring to appendices; noting the connectives. The ability to use all of these elements to aid understanding.
- **Being aware of effect on the reader** – the habit of being aware of the author's intention. This creates a strong link to exploring structure and effect and noticing how a writer creates an impact.
- **Summarising** – the habit of pulling together the main threads of a text. In some cases, with a complicated argument or information, this might involve pausing and summarising every section and then re-reading to get a view of the whole picture.
- **Evaluating** – the habit of being able to read appreciatively and with discrimination. Being able to judge and justify which text has more merit and explain why.

Children need to be able to orchestrate the full range of these reading habits to enjoy and get the most out of what they read until they become an automatic part of their reading 'toolkit'.

Where texts are demanding, children will need to **'read strategically'**, turning up the volume of different aspects of being a reader to aid their understanding. Across a Talk for Reading unit, the full range of reading comprehension habits will be modelled and practised. However, different texts may well demand different aspects of reading to sharpen the teaching.

4. Preparing for the three phases of Talk for Reading

Before getting into the detail of the teaching (see **Chapters 3**, **4 & 5**), it is important to familiarise ourselves with the three phases of Talk for Reading and think about how to prepare for these appropriately.

The Introduction Phase

This first phase involves reading the text a number of times so that the children develop a basic understanding of the text.

Throughout this phase, you model reading the text aloud with fluency, encouraging children to listen, join in or imitate chorally, as appropriate. Whilst introducing the text to the class, you can also be:

- drawing on background information or experiences;
- predicting, e.g. from the cover or opening/end of the text;
- taking initial responses and ideas;
- exploring vocabulary in the context of the text;
- retrieving literal information and understanding;
- establishing significant themes, questions or lines of enquiry to focus and fuel further discussion.

The Introduction Phase

Achieve basic understanding:

Before reading
- hook;
- context;
- activate prior knowledge.

While reading
- teacher models reading with fluency;
- prediction;
- initial responses;
- re-reading;
- initial vocabulary;
- literal retrieval;
- establish focus.

I posted the following on social media.

> ***"Continually stopping on each page when reading to children to ask questions, etc. may well make comprehension harder for any child with a weak short-term memory as they cannot hold what has happened and create the links needed to build a global model."***

This seemed to resonate with thousands of teachers. Someone even pointed out how adverts interrupt a programme; another suggested how annoying it would be if you were reading a book and someone kept making you stop to discuss it at the end of every page! As teachers, we feel obliged to be constantly 'teaching' and the habit of pausing on every page of a picture book is well intentioned, but may make the act of comprehension more difficult. To build that global model – to get the big picture or enter the story world – the reading should not be interrupted. Too many long pauses mean that for some children the threads unravel, key aspects get forgotten and the text no longer coheres. This is especially true for any children with a weaker short-term memory. The first read-through needs to be without pause so that the text creates the spell. We suggest that during a unit the text is re-read just so that the children can re-experience the text as a whole, adding in new understandings to the reading. If the text is any good, the class will demand to have it again anyway! The **Introduction Phase** is explored in more depth in **Chapter 3**.

The Investigation Phase

In this phase, the reading should be slowed right down to begin to build the habit of reading strategically, closely and thoughtfully. During this stage, the children will be increasingly clarifying their understanding which will inevitably involve moving from reading at a literal level to inferring from the text to build an increasingly sophisticated picture. This needs careful thought and planning. You should consider these questions.

> **The Investigation Phase**
>
> Deepen understanding of the focus through:
>
> - oral comprehension;
> - strategic reading;
> - response activities;
> - exploring structure and effect;
> - summarising;
> - evaluating;
> - reading fluently.

- *What questions will open discussion? What questions will scaffold understanding? What questions will encourage children to think more deeply?*
- *What strategic approach might be needed to develop understanding of this text? How might I model being a reader?*

- *What response activities will deepen understanding? Could drama or writing-in-role build more emotional engagement?*
- *Which section could be used to explore structure and effect? How is the language used in the chosen section to create the effect? Would writing in the style of the writer support understanding? Is it appropriate or too sophisticated as a model?*
- *Could a story map be created or the text boxed-up to see the structure and summarise the content?*
- *How might the children summarise their learning? What scaffold might they need in order to respond to the text and clarify their thinking?*
- *How will children evaluate the text?*
- *Will the children perform this text chorally? Will they re-read it in paragraphs as groups, or independently re-read a well-rehearsed section using expression?*

Anyone can dream up 30 activities to do with a text. The skill is to focus on those activities and discussions that will help children understand the whole text, as well as investigate the chosen concepts. The **Investigation Phase** is explored in more depth in **Chapter 4**.

The Independent Understanding Phase

By the end of the **Independent Understanding Phase**, children should be in a position to demonstrate independent understanding, as outlined in **Chapter 5**.

There are various ways in which understanding might be demonstrated.

The Independent Understanding Phase

Demonstrate understanding through:

- talking or writing as a reader about the core text; or
- identifying the key focus in another text and responding; or
- applying what they have learned in their own writing.

- *Can the children demonstrate understanding of the core text through talking or writing as a reader?*
- *Can the children identify the key focus in another similar text, explore discursively and respond?*
- *Can the children apply what they have learned by drawing on their reading to write something similar?*

5. Teaching the text

Now that you've chosen a great text, or cluster of texts, and selected the comprehension focus/es, you can think about how to approach teaching. It is essential that we consider vocabulary because, if the children do not understand the words, then comprehension becomes impossible.

Vocabulary

Research clearly shows that poor vocabulary is a prime cause of academic failure. Words are slippery things as the meaning can change depending on context (e.g. *pitch*); or intonation (e.g. *Marvellous!*). They can also be totally reliant on world knowledge. Words, of course, fit into sentences, so often it is the phrase, clause or sentence that needs considering.

Since there are too many words to teach directly, it's important to plan which words to teach explicitly. In the main, the meaning of the words gradually becomes clearer during the class discussions. A useful strategy is to ask children to highlight and identify and words or phrases that 'need discussing'.

For most units, you need to select about a dozen or so key words that are vital to the deep meaning of the text, often linked to the pinch points. This will also include words and phrases that you want the children to add to their vocabulary. These can be displayed on a washing line, usually accompanied by an image or icon to remind children of the meaning, as shown in the picture below taken from a Year 2 washing line at Penn Wood Primary School in Slough.

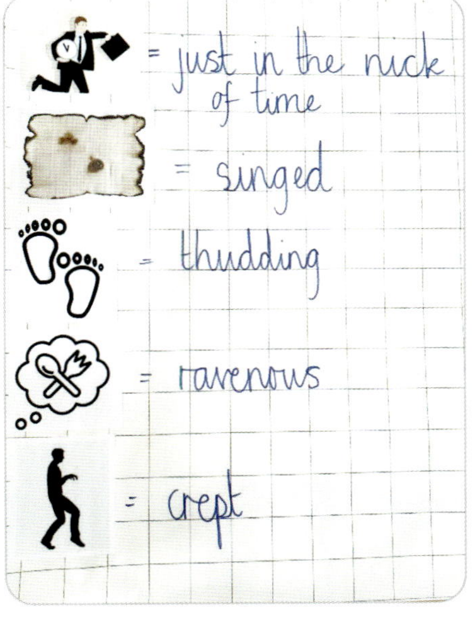

Activities should then be carried out to provide child-friendly definitions. It's important for children to repeat the definition and word, before experimenting with deepening understanding of how the word is used – and, most importantly, using it in new sentences.

Planning discussion points and key questions

One of the things that I loved as a teacher of reading is deciding where in the text a discussion might be needed. This might be:

- **before** starting the text;
- **during** reading the text;
- **after** reading the text;
- **revisiting** sections of the text.

Discussions can be started by open invitation to comment.

- *What can we say about the text so far?*
- *What matters here?*
- *Anyone got any thoughts about this?*

This approach can be very helpful as it often suggests what the children are interested in or where the class has not quite understood. Very often, the key discussions are around clarifying what has happened or what has been learned so far. Be ready to listen to the children and pick up on different ideas and views.

With complex texts, it can be helpful to chunk it up into sections that need to be understood. In this way, a line of argument can be more clearly followed; information or viewpoints grasped and scenes or verses linked cumulatively to build comprehension. Try boxing the text up to help children summarise 'so far'. Build the text up piece by piece. Model this on the first few chunks by thinking aloud and explaining what you are doing. Then involve the children, co-constructing meaning before letting them loose on the final sections prior to feeding back and trying to assemble the big overview. Display key points on flipchart pages so that you can build a picture of the text on the wall.

You could also try using statements to start the discussions, such as these examples.

- *Macbeth is a flawed character.*
- *The Iron Man is a good character.*
- *Varjak Paw learns nothing.*
- *The poet sympathises with the highwayman who is an immoral character.*
- *Greta Thunberg overstates her case.*
- *Tom never went back in time as a ghost; he was dreaming.*
- *Small children need to learn to put up with disappointments such as losing a toy.*

As a tutor, I once observed a student holding a book session and counted the number of questions she asked. She read the story well, but then bombarded the children with 63 closed questions in just over 20 minutes. Of course, the responses veered towards one-word answers, so no extended thinking was happening. The children either knew the answer or did not. For those who did not know the answer, it confirmed that they were no good at 'comprehension' and the session helped no one.

Over the years, I have built up a sense of the sort of questions that are helpful to ask and their purposes.

- There will be small **'checking questions'** that help you check in with the class that they are following the text.
- There may be questions that help **scaffold understanding**, e.g. we need to know what happened at the start of the short story in order to understand why a character behaved in a certain way later on.
- There will also be questions that help children think about what has happened in a more **critical** manner, e.g. *is the writer biased?*
- **Open questions** that invite discussion. These are best used when children are not trying to guess what is in your head, but feel free to 'think aloud'. This enables them to 'think deeply' and 'follow trains of thought' and, over time, becomes an established, automatic reading habit. Open questions should invite extended answers where children feel free to speculate.
- **Focused questions** for directing the children to think more carefully about key areas that might have been missed or glossed over.
- **Closed questions** for checking understanding. If there are misconceptions, it can be helpful to **follow up** by asking children to explain and justify their thoughts using evidence from the text.

The main intention of questioning is not to 'test' the children, but to invite them to think deeply about the text, so that in the end they develop the habit of reading in a questioning manner. Our starting point as teachers is to show interest in what the children are thinking and understanding.

Identify a key area for exploration, usually related to the core literary concepts. This is often framed as a 'Big Question' to give a focus to each unit. We have found that this can be tricky and is often best done in collaboration with other teachers.

Areas of focus for a section of *The Iron Man* might be framed in different ways.

- *Considering the opening and ending, is the Iron Man the hero?*
- *Explore whether the main character is the Iron Man or Hogarth.*
- *How does the way in which the opening is written hook the reader?*
- *How effectively does Ted Hughes portray the Iron Man and the Dragon?*

I have seen teachers bedevilled by overcomplicated formats for questioning. One that inevitably never worked for me is *Bloom's Taxonomy*, which was initially not meant for teaching purposes, but developed to help test makers create questions of varying difficulty. The idea looked good and sounded promising, but I was never bright enough to make much use of it. The key problem with trying to use complicated taxonomies and question types is that invariably they are too difficult to retain and therefore of little use. They create an illusion of something sophisticated that make the management team feel their approach is at the cutting edge. However, in 40 years of education, I have never known complex taxonomies to genuinely be of use to everyday teaching.

I'm tempted to say that only a mad person ignores national testing regimes. However, for real lasting understanding and progression, you need more than just teaching to the test. The skill is to be familiar with the test, understand the sorts of questions that come up and how they are framed and weave this into your regular teaching across each key stage – without ruining the teaching.

6. Assessing and supporting individual readers who struggle

Whilst Talk for Reading is focused on developing comprehension, successful schools ensure that they know their children as readers, beyond test scores and reading ages. Standardised test results are only the product of a child's competence to comprehend the specific text that they have just read. They don't always tell the whole story, especially for children who struggle to comprehend. If an answer is *wrong*, there may well be multiple reasons for this.

Two children who fail to give a correct response to a particular question may well have very different reasons. It could be:

- problems with sight, hearing or speech;
- anxiety about reading, poor self-image as a reader and poor motivation;
- inability to decode;
- slow rate of reading;

- lack of fluency and expression;
- lack of reading stamina with longer texts;
- being confronted with unfamiliar words, archaic language, metaphorical phrases or tricky unknown references;
- poor comprehension monitoring skills;
- an inability to hold information in the working memory while reading;
- an inability to infer between sentences and across texts;
- a lack of world knowledge or experience of the subject matter;
- or they may simply not have been motivated to read the text!

We need to draw on a variety of information to assess what children know and can do and where they might need to go next to develop as readers. Successful schools plan in assessment opportunities by hearing children read aloud and discussing their reading with them. This enables teachers to understand the child's preferences as a reader and assess their fluency and understanding. Consider using the following questions as a starting point.

- *Do children attempt unfamiliar words by using phonics?*
- *Do they re-read and self-correct if the word doesn't 'sound right' or the sentence or phrase doesn't make sense?*
- *Do they read on and around an unfamiliar word to try and make sense?*
- *Can they use their growing knowledge of roots, prefixes and suffixes attempt new words?*
- *Are they able to read at a reasonable rate, accurately and effortlessly?*
- *Can they read aloud with fluency and expression, taking account of the punctuation?*

When returning to a text, consider the questions below for readers who struggle.

- *Can they make links across a text, e.g. keep track of the pronouns?*
- *Are they able to locate specific information by scanning the text?*
- *Can they explain the gist of a text?*
- *Do they draw on experiences and wider knowledge to make sense of what they are reading?*
- *Can they paraphrase what they have read in their own words?*
- *Are they able to summarise the main points in a text?*

Having a system for regularly hearing children read aloud individually, taking an interest in them as readers and their reading development is key to effective planning, teaching and feedback.

In essence, we need to be tracking the children's decoding, word recognition, reading rate, fluency and comprehension. With children of concern, this will be more regular than the majority who might have such a conference every half-term. This information will tell the school who needs more teaching and practice and in what aspects of reading. Concerns need picking up as soon as possible before failure becomes a habit. Some children may need one-to-one support, though all our successful schools also use guided reading so that children who need similar teaching, read at a similar level or need a similar challenge are taught in a group. It is essential that anyone involved in guided/group reading at any stage is an expert in reading. Those involved must receive training and feedback so that they can deepen their subject knowledge and teach reading effectively. These sessions are not just 'hearing reading' round the table.

In a sense, this is separate from Talk for Reading, but using assessment of an individual's reading development and acting upon it, is an essential part of ensuring whole school transformation.

Chapter 3: The Introduction Phase

Achieve basic understanding

Pie Corbett

> **The Introduction Phase**
>
> Achieve basic understanding:
>
> **Before reading**
> - hook;
> - context;
> - activate prior knowledge.
>
> **While reading**
> - teacher models reading with fluency;
> - prediction;
> - initial responses;
> - re-reading;
> - initial vocabulary;
> - literal retrieval;
> - establish focus.

By the end of this first teaching phase, the children need to be fairly confident at reading the text with some ease, having thought through the vocabulary. It is impossible to comprehend the meaning of the text if they don't understand the words. For younger children, they will need to listen to the text being read to them as their decoding and word recognition skills will be behind their ability to comprehend.

While the various aspects of the **Introduction Phase** are set out here in a linear fashion (see blue box), it may well be that different aspects happen on different days and in a different order. That will be determined by the demands of the text as well as the confidence of the class. The starting point is that you have selected a high-quality text, or texts, that will be of interest to the class, pitched well above the reading level of the children to help develop thoughtful reading (see **Chapter 2**).

1. Before reading

Hook

The idea of the 'hook' arose from working on the Talk for Writing process. Children write best about what they know and what matters to them. Teachers began inventing interesting ways to launch writing units of work with first-hand experiences, visits and visitors, drama, film clips, letters arriving and mysterious boxes appearing. For writing, the ideal hook generates engagement and sets up a strong sense of audience and purpose. If a teaching assistant in Year 1 has made the error of climbing the beanstalk and has been captured by the giant, then begging letters must be written to the giant! All of this is just play, but it does give a strong sense of purpose to the learning.

So, what would we use as a hook for reading? How do we set up curiosity and draw children into reading with a sense of purpose? Sometimes, the text alone is sufficient and we can just launch straight into a dramatic reading. All of this depends on the text, but here are a series of creative possibilities.

- **A quick teaser** – stimulate curiosity by showing an image, object, film clip, title, front cover, author interview, blurb from the back of the book, the middle pages from a picture book, or a chosen line to trigger discussion and wondering.
- **Story museum/text box** – reveal key items from the story, e.g. leaves, twigs, a red hat, magical beans, a cow's horn, etc.
- **Written/spoken documents** – leave some writing lying around relating to the text for the children to 'discover'. It could be a letter about rumours of a Minotaur, a diary entry about an Iron Man, a newspaper report about an everlasting winter or an email or blog by a character from the story you are going to be working on. Alternatively, you could record a film message for the children to watch. The film could feature a character from a story or have information about the text content.
- **A request** – perhaps someone needs help and the children have to read a message in order to assist them. For example, Dr Who might need information about a planet. This sets up a purpose for reading which can help children read in a more focused manner.

Hooking the reader should not become self-indulgent and eat up swathes of time. There is no need to convert the central area into Narnia! A teasing opening that raises curiosity may well only take a few minutes.

Context

A good novel generally works without prior information, though there may be occasions where some texts benefit from contextual knowledge to enhance and deepen understanding. For instance, *The Jolly Postman* by Janet and Allan Ahlberg will not have the full impact unless the reader is familiar with the fairy tales that it references. De la Mare's *The Listeners* will have less of an effect on children who have never stood in a forest. Lindsay Galvin's *Darwin's Dragons* is enhanced by a little information about Darwin. *Floodland* by Marcus Sedgwick makes more sense if the children know about what might happen to sea levels with global warming. This information, plus a map of the area and images of Ely Cathedral, would all enhance the story. *Hatchet* by Gary Paulsen is easier to visualise if the children have seen a short film clip of the terrain where the story is set.

Many schools use a cluster of related or paired texts (sometimes known as 'satellite texts') to enrich the reading of the core text. In some instances basic contextual information may be useful, but for a richer reading, texts that run alongside each other may be most helpful when they deepen understanding of key concepts or themes. An extra text could provide:

- background facts (see the image here of notes written by a teacher, as an introduction to Romantic Poetry, before reading *A Poison Tree* by William Blake);
- a similar text type;
- an exploration of a key theme;
- another example of a key literary concept.

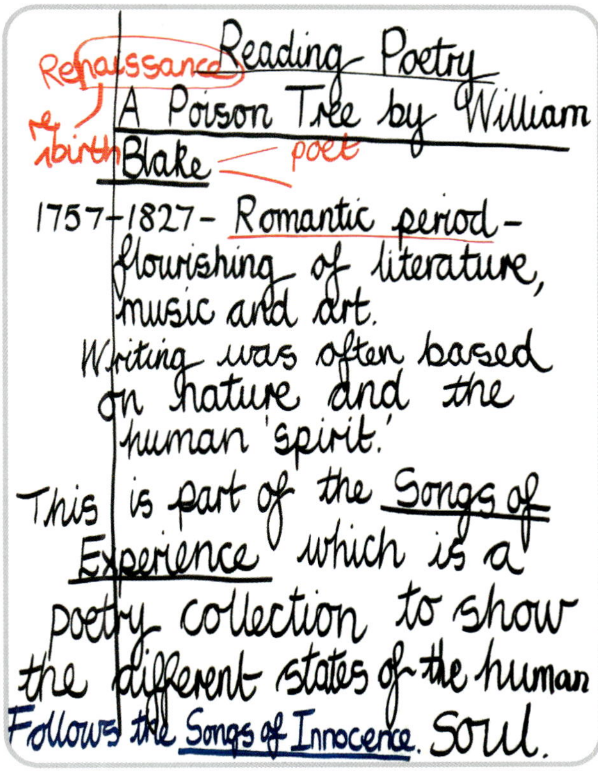

A book such as *Good Little Wolf* by Nadia Shireen, almost entirely hangs around children knowing about wolves in fairy stories, especially their penchant for eating grandmothers and children! The end just doesn't work unless children are familiar with *Little Red Riding Hood* and *The Three Little Pigs*. Linking Shaun Tan's *The Arrival* to historical work on refugees adds an extra layer of interpretation in the same way that Blake's *The Tyger* opens up if you have shared a text about the industrial revolution with the class. *The Owl Who Was Afraid of the Dark* by Jill Tomlinson doesn't make much sense if you do not know that owls hunt at night. Therefore, reading a non-fiction book about owls alongside it, could be helpful for children.

Activate prior knowledge

It may well be important to activate prior knowledge when introducing a text. *What do the class already know about this theme, subject or type of text?* A good opening session might involve spending some time activating knowledge and setting up some reading expectations – what we expect from the text; what we need from the text; what we know about the main subject; what the author might have needed to know to write this text. This might involve activating subject or textual knowledge. Or it could be focused on a theme such as, 'times we have been lonely', to tune the children into the theme of a story so that they can bring what they know from their own experience to make connections with a character.

We have often used the picture book *On Sudden Hill* by Linda Sarah in the early years. In this book, two children spend a lot of time playing with boxes which they pretend are castles, robots or vehicles. Early in the story, another child joins them with his box. This upsets the rhythm of the initial friendship. Of course, it is fun to bring boxes into the classroom to generate ideas for play in the preceding weeks, but is the book actually about boxes? To get the most from the book, discussions or reading books about friendship, jealousy, coping with negative feelings and accepting someone new – so that 'three' isn't a crowd – would be more helpful. It's useful for the children to think about the 'theme' of the book – what is it really about? Is *The Billy Goats Gruff* about goats? Is *The Three Pigs* about piglets? Is *Charlotte's Web* about spiders and pigs?

The other key aspect to think carefully about is whether there needs to be some prior teaching of vocabulary. When planning your unit of work, ask yourself if there are any key words without which the whole meaning falls apart. Remember to keep this limited because the new vocabulary is best taught gradually over the **Introduction Phase** of reading, in context.

The concern about over-egging vocabulary before reading is that children need to develop the ability to use the context as they read to become independent readers. They need to learn to use context to get the gist, but also recognise where meaning has fallen apart and know how to draw on other resources, e.g. a dictionary, to find out what a key word or concept means.

2. While reading

Teacher models reading with fluency

On an initial reading, it is important to use your best teacher 'reading voice', dramatising the reading with expression. This is worth thinking about, because in our haste to 'teach comprehension', the key aim of reading can get lost – which is to develop a love of reading through being able to read confidently and fluently with deep understanding and critical appreciation. Initially, just read the text to the children for the pleasure of the experience. However, remember that during this initial read is the only time **prediction** can happen (see below).

Prediction

It is worth thinking carefully about where to pause for a moment of prediction as too many pauses ruin the flow of a text. The key places will be where there is information in the part of the text that has just been read that suggests what might happen next. In that way, we can work on 'informed' predictions, rather than wild guessing.

To avoid pausing during the first read-through, you could predict from the cover, the blurb or even from chapter headings. Some texts also lend themselves to predicting at the end of the book what might happen next to the characters. It is worth remembering that you DO NOT have to do prediction every time and, indeed, as children become more proficient at reading thoughtfully, it may well not be necessary.

Even when taking steps to ensure children's predictions are informed, there will still be occasions when they make 'wild' guesses about what is going to unfold in the text. These are the sort of predictions that might be possible, but bare very little relation to the text or what we know of life. In these cases, we need to train the children to think about 'what is most likely' using prediction question stems, like those below, related to clues in the text. Prediction is more than a hunch. Certainly, in any form of test situation, where children are asked to predict, the relevant passage will contain clues that can be used to suggest what might happen next.

Initially, children will need help with the vocabulary, phrasing and thinking that underpin logical prediction. Below is some of the vocabulary and phrasing that will need modelling.

Prediction vocabulary

predict	implies	suggests
indicates	forecast	surmise
conclude that	because	therefore

Prediction question stems

- *Do you think that [a character] will change their behaviour? Find one or two pieces of evidence.*
- *What may have happened before/previously/beforehand/earlier...? [Insert an event from the text.]*
- *What possibly could happen next/later/afterwards/because of/as a consequence of/as a result of/following...? [Insert an event from the text.]*
- *Referring to the text, what do you think will happen next/because of/as a consequence of/as a result of...? [Insert an event/action from the text.]*
- *Based on what we know so far, how do you think [character/s] will react/change/alter/respond when...? [Insert an event from the text.]*

Prediction answer stems

- *I predict that...*
- *I know this because in the text it states...*
- *This suggests that...*

Video clip 1 shows me modelling and teaching prediction in Year 1.

Initial responses

After the first read-through, you can take **initial responses** which, over time, can be built upon. This is a chance for the children to talk in pairs, groups and as a class about their experience of the text. It is quite natural after any big experience to discuss preferences. After watching a film, we might discuss what we liked and didn't like; what might have worked better; why the characters behaved in certain ways; what it reminded us of, etc. The same applies to something we have read. At this stage, what is discussed very much depends on what arises from the children and the type of text that has been shared.

To get children into the habit of thinking through their responses and noticing their own reactions, you might just ask, *"What do you want to say about this text?"* They may need a few prompts to get them used to talking through their experience of the text.

- *What did you like about this?*
- *Was there anything that you didn't like?*
- *What did it remind you of?*
- *What memories did it trigger?*
- *How did it make you feel?*
- *Which character did you connect with?*
- *What interested you most?*
- *What surprised you?*
- *What was new to you?*
- *What do you think is the most important thing in this text?*
- *What links can you make – with your life/other books?*
- *What are you uncertain about?*
- *What would you ask the author?*
- *What did you think of the ending?*

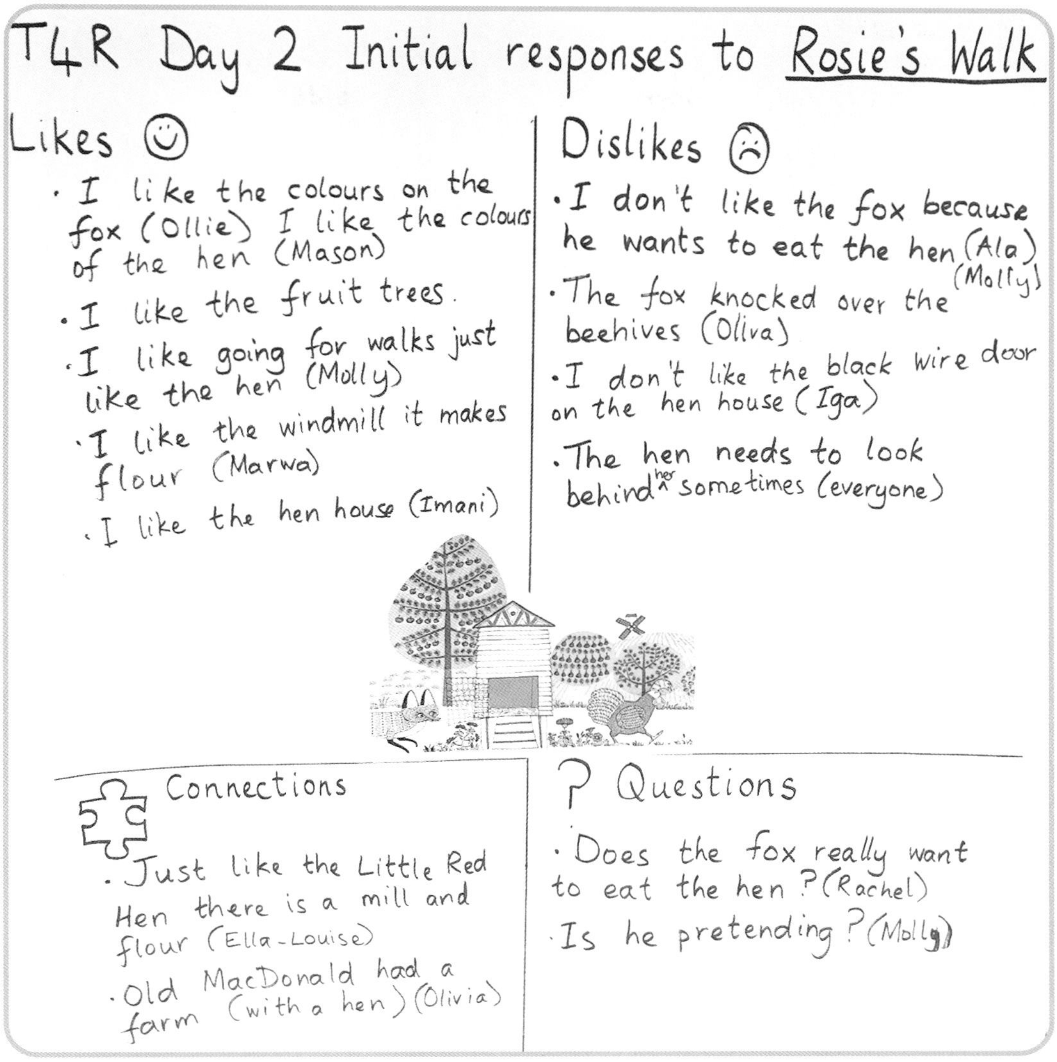

One way to capture initial responses is to use a ‘booktalk grid’. This concept takes inspiration from the work of Aidan Chambers in his seminal work, *Tell Me* (Thimble Press). We revisit this in greater detail in the **Investigation Phase**.

To do this with younger children, you could initiate a conversation with them about what they liked and disliked about the story, as well as inviting them to make any connections to other texts and talk about any questions they would like to raise.

The image above illustrates the responses of a Reception class at Briar Hill Primary School, following their initial reading of *Rosie’s Walk* by Pat Hutchins.

This next extract from a flipchart page shows the initial responses to the prologue of *The Snow Walker's Son* by Catherine Fisher. The discussions encouraged children to talk about what surprised them, what wonders they have, what they predict will happen next and any connections they are able to make with wider literature. These categories need to be chosen to reflect the text potential, as they open up initial thought that can then be revisited and developed across the unit of work.

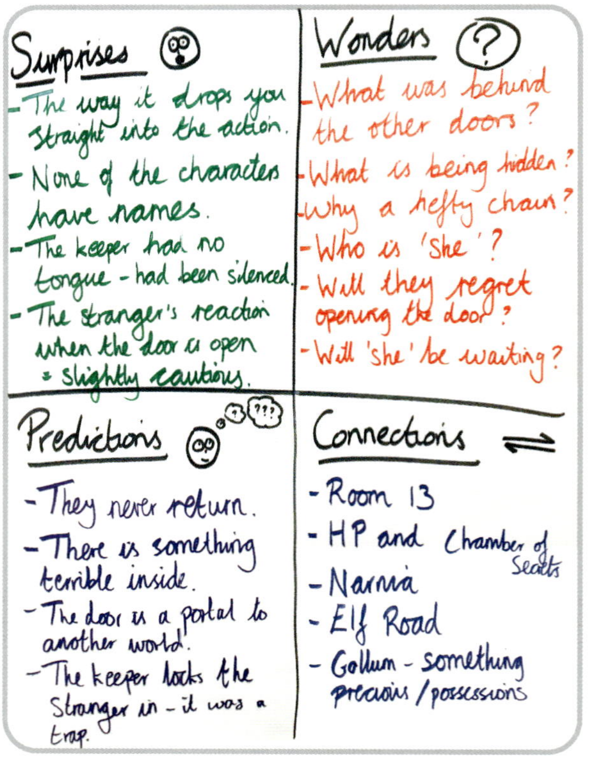

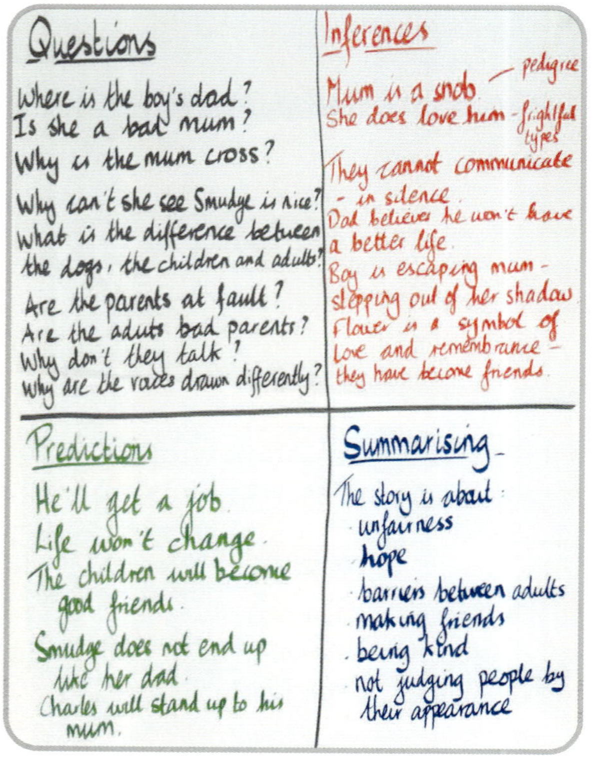

Finally, this image shows initial responses collected on a flipchart to *Voices in the Park* by Anthony Browne. The grid identifies questions to explore further, inferences, predictions and some suggestions by children about their thoughts on the main theme.

The idea is that when a child makes a response, it is not just written up and then you move on to the next response. There should be a rich discussion with the children doing most of the talking and you orchestrating the conversation. With an experienced class, this will already begin to deepen understanding as ideas are shared.

As a teacher, it is important to be a good listener, encouraging children, repeating ideas that might need thinking about, and occasionally challenging them by asking for further explanation or justification. I often find myself saying, *"That's interesting, has anyone else got anything to add to that idea or is there another way of looking at it?"* Sometimes, it is worth pushing children by focusing them where there is more to say, *"I think there might be more here.*

Let's re-read it and then you can discuss in pairs before we share together." Occasionally, it is worth being even more specific, *"I think there are three things that we might comment on here."*

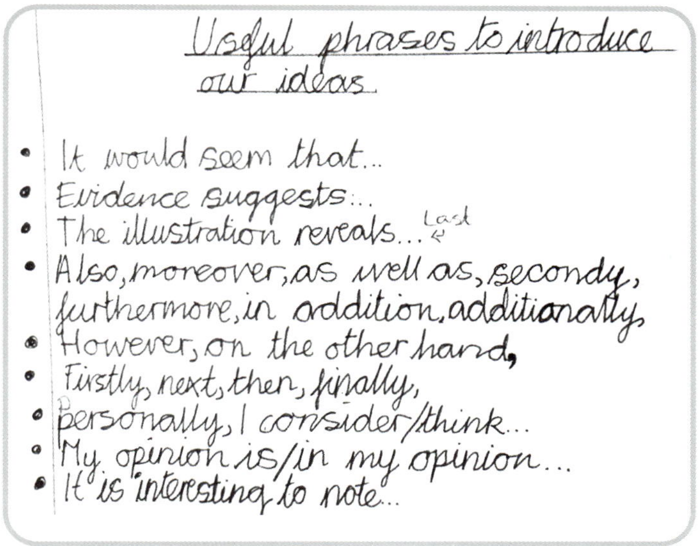

Useful phrases to introduce our ideas

- It would seem that...
- Evidence suggests...
- The illustration reveals...
- Also, moreover, as well as, secondy, furthermore, in addition, additionally,
- However, on the other hand,
- Firstly, next, then, finally,
- personally, I consider/think...
- My opinion is/in my opinion...
- It is interesting to note...

It is important to listen very carefully to 'how' a child puts something and praise good habits, e.g. building on what someone else has said, using technical reading language (*"by comparison"* or *"this symbolises"*). It helps to list vocabulary and phrases that might be useful when holding discussions. The image on the left shows a list written by a Year 5 pupil, with suggestions of useful phrases for their discussion.

Older children, at KS2, benefit from using their 'magpie' books to jot down their initial thoughts during the first reading, before discussing it as a class. This could be to note themes they wish to explore, points they want to make and to capture important lines or vocabulary. If the children have a photocopy of the text, they can annotate it during or just after reading the text, to help them gather their ideas. The notes in the 'magpie' book can then be added to during the class discussions, as shown here.

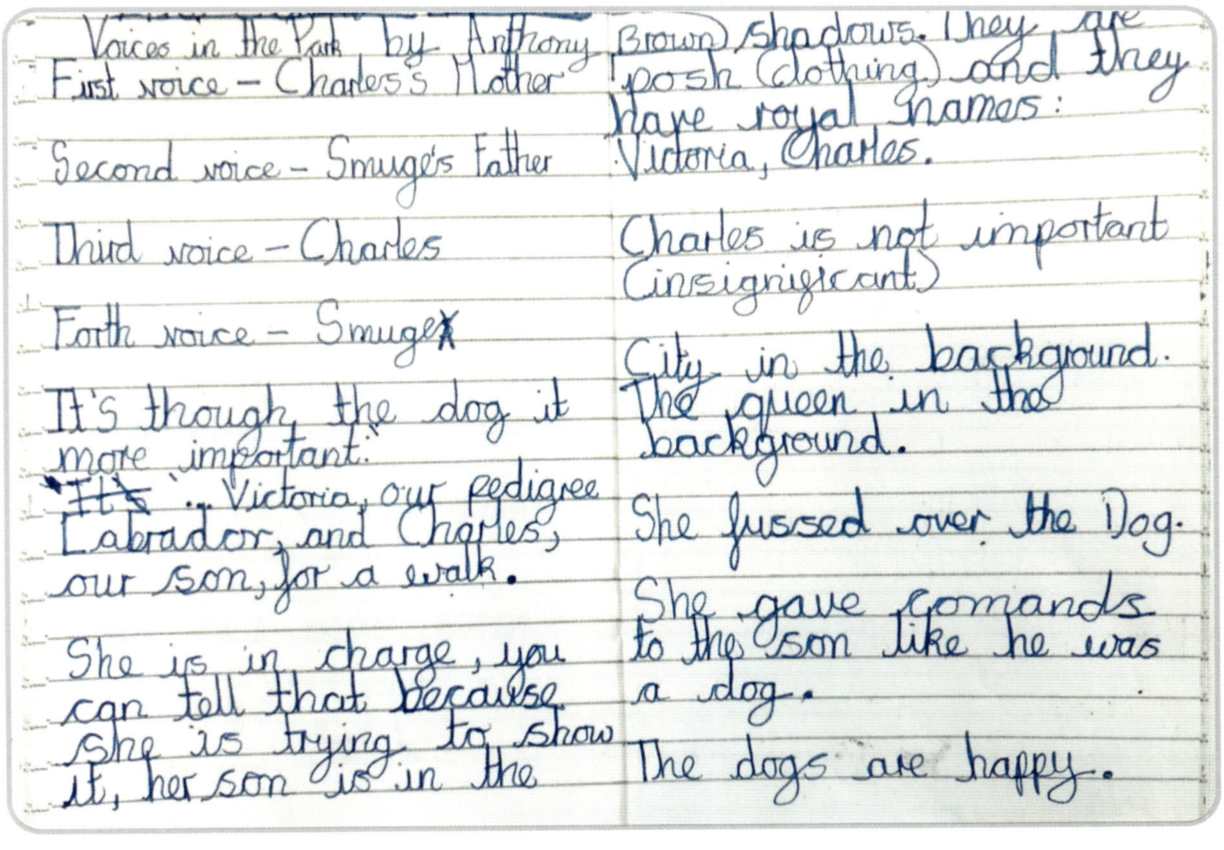

Voices in the Park by Anthony Brown
First voice – Charles's Mother
Second voice – Smuge's Father
Third voice – Charles
Forth voice – Smuge
It's though the dog it more important:
"... Victoria, our pedigree Labrador, and Charles, our son, for a walk.
She is in charge, you can tell that because she is trying to show it, her son is in the shadows. They are posh (clothing) and they have royal names: Victoria, Charles.
Charles is not important (insignificant)
City in the background. The queen in the background.
She fussed over the Dog.
She gave comands to the son like he was a dog.
The dogs are happy.

After discussions have taken place, older children can move into formal writing to capture their ideas. This would need to be modelled using shared writing, with sentence stems also provided to help structure ideas.

- *My first thoughts were…*
- *I thought this because…*
- *The best section was…*
- *I was shocked to find out that…*
- *After the discussion, I realised that…*
- *I liked how…*
- *I didn't really understand why…*
- *I never knew that…*
- *I was surprised to find out that…*
- *I still don't understand why…*

Here, you can see an initial response to the penultimate page in *Voices in the Park* by a Year 6 child. Other pages had been discussed, but the teacher asked the children to write about the last few pages.

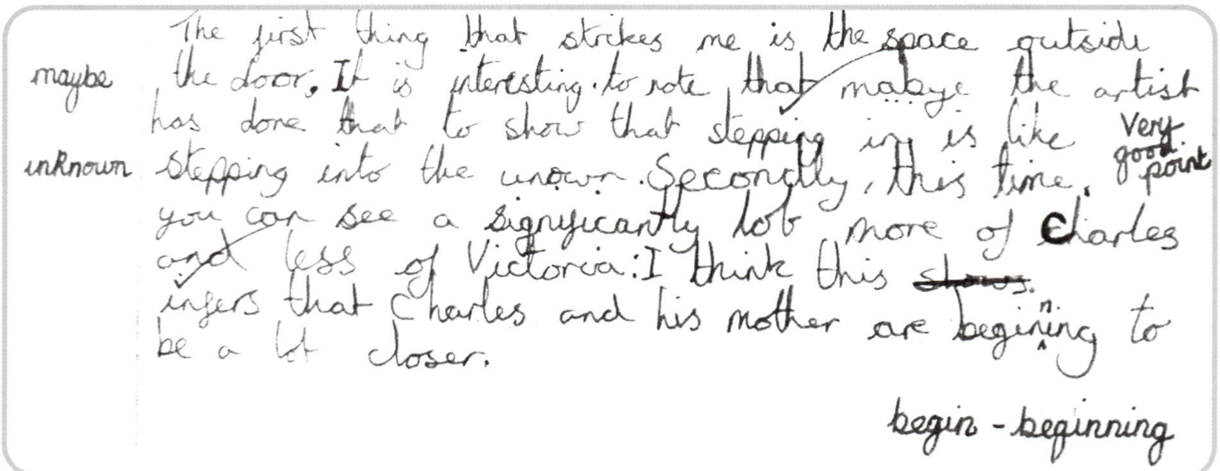

See **Handout 1 (online)** for further examples of sentence stems and comprehension grids to support initial responses.

There are, of course, many other ways to share, explore and deepen initial responses. You could ask the children to have a go at any of the following activities.

- *In silence, spend three minutes writing down what moved you/surprised you/it reminded you of in your life/you would say to the main character. Talk about what you have written in pairs before coming together as a class to share ideas.*
- *Sketch the main scene that stayed with you.*
- *Select one fact, idea or argument to discuss.*

- *Which word, phrase or sentence struck you the most and why? Share your chosen words with the class.*
- *Write a note to your favourite character and be ready to share it with the class.*
- *Sit back-to-back with a partner and have a pretend phone call to a chosen character for a post-story discussion about what has happened.*
- *Best and Worst – list the best things and worst things about the text and share your ideas.*

Re-reading

As the aim of this first phase is to establish basic confidence with reading the text and comprehension, albeit at a superficial level, a number of re-readings will be necessary. The first read through will be for the pleasure of hearing it read with expression and fluency. At this point we can also gather initial responses, thoughts and opinions. Subsequent readings will support children in securing a basic understanding of the text. This may include clarifying the meaning of key vocabulary within context , before venturing into literal retrieval. **Video clip 2** shows Jamie modelling explicit vocabulary teaching and gathering initial responses in Year 2 with one of my stories, *Kassim and the Greedy Dragon*.

Initial vocabulary

During this first phase, key vocabulary can be attended to and discussed. A simple explanation might be enough for some words. However, there may be key terms that are essential to understanding the text that need to be given more attention. The children should also be involved in identifying tricky vocabulary (for older ones, this might mean text marking the words and phrases that need discussing). As teachers, we tend to make assumptions that children know more than they sometimes do. For instance, there was a Year 1 class in a city school that were uncertain about what the word 'town' meant!

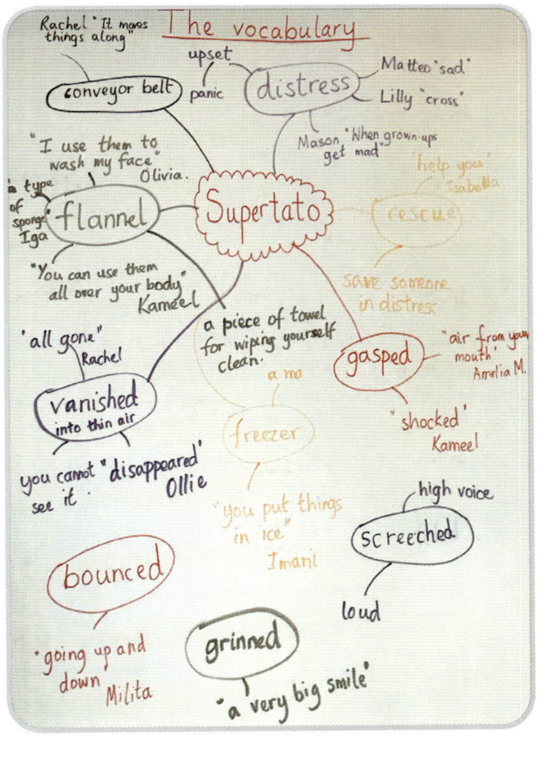

Without killing the text, vocabulary work can be built in with a little bit each day over the **Introduction Phase**. Some of this might be addressed through discussion, with key words listed and defined in 'magpie' books or on a flipchart, as the image here from Briar Hill Primary School illustrates.

Other words may benefit from the full

teaching routine that involves repeating a child-friendly definition, saying the word aloud, using activities to deepen understanding and finally trying the word in sentences (see **video clips 3 & 4**). It is worth remembering that we all gradually deepen our understanding of vocabulary through constantly meeting words within a context and, thereby, shaping the subtleties of meaning and the possibilities of use.

Literal retrieval

By this point in the **Introduction Phase**, the children should have a rudimentary understanding of the text and its meaning, so it is a good time to carry out some basic work on literal retrieval. This can be at a fairly simple level where they just have to re-read a sentence and find basic information, e.g. "*What colour were the giant's eyes?*" More challenging, for many, will be trying to locate where information or ideas are in different places within a text that have to be collated together.

Here are some simple starting points for literal retrieval.

- *Find two/three things that you are told about...*
- *Find the three/four facts about...*
- *What did [a character] have to do in order to...?*
- *What was revealed at the beginning/middle/end of the story?*
- *Which of these statements is true or false...?*
- *A character does something. Provide four choices of 'how' adverbs not explicitly stated in the text.*
- *Everything was fine... until... Provide a choice of four events.*
- *Give two reasons why [a character] was [insert mood]... before... [an event].*
- *What is the main reason given for...?*
- *Give one/two reasons why/how [an event] happened.*
- *Why did [a character] do something [event previously stated in text]?*
- *Look at page... Give one piece of [advice/information] that [a character] gives [another character].*
- *We are told three pieces of information about... List them.*

Early on, it is helpful to model using some straightforward sentence starters for discussions.

- *In the text, it tells us that...*
- *The author states that...*
- *In the third paragraph, it says...*
- *The text tells us that...*
- *There are... [insert number] points that we know. It states...*

Establish key focus

When you feel that the children are ready, core questions, enquiries, challenges or 'big questions' can be established to draw this first phase to an end. Some of these focuses may have arisen during the initial responses or developed as the text is re-read. The children may well have identified areas to explore further.

These can be discussed in pairs or small groups, by asking the children to raise:

- questions worth discussing;
- things they are not sure about;
- things that need more investigation or discussion.

As a teacher, you should also have a key comprehension focus (or several focuses) for the unit of work and have thought through a core question, enquiry or challenge, depending on the demands of the text and any aspects of literary understanding it lends itself to. For instance, not every narrative is suitable for a focus on exploring 'viewpoint'. Enquiries should be based around key literary concepts which together contribute to understanding the **purpose of the text** (see **page 16**).

Core questions or reading challenges provide a steer for the next phase where the text is investigated in more depth.

Here is a list of example enquiry questions based on the key literary concepts.

- *In this chapter, what sort of character is Tom portrayed as and how does he differ from other people's views?* (***The Midnight Fox*** by Betsy Byars)
- *In this article, what do we know about the author's viewpoint and how is this revealed?*
- *What does the Tyger symbolise compared to the Lamb? What is the role of the Blacksmith?* (***The Tyger*** by William Blake)
- *Is Tim the ostler a hero?* (***The Highwayman*** by Alfred Noyes)
- *Explain how the writer is biased and the potential effect on the reader?*
- *What does the article tell us about different views about global warming and which do you think is best argued?*
- *Who is worse – Lady Macbeth or her husband?* (***Macbeth*** by William Shakespeare)

This image shows a page from a Year 6 child's English book where she has listed features about the story that have been noticed, summarising the class discussion.

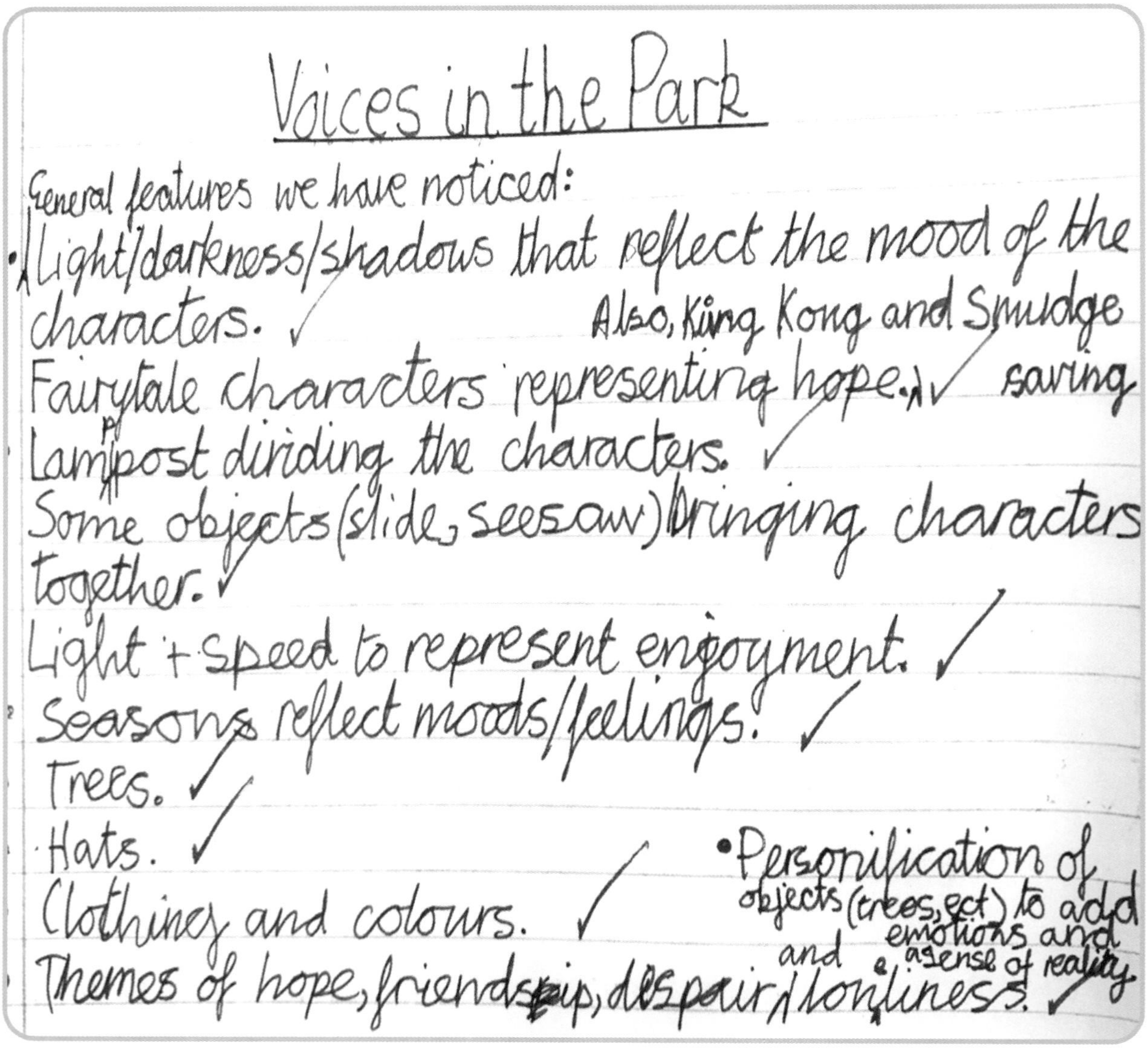

Voices in the Park

General features we have noticed:

- Light/darkness/shadows that reflect the mood of the characters.
- Fairytale characters representing hope. Also, King Kong and Smudge saving
- Lampost dividing the characters.
- Some objects (slide, seesaw) bringing characters together.
- Light + speed to represent enjoyment.
- Seasons reflect moods/feelings.
- Trees.
- Hats.
- Clothing and colours.
- Themes of hope, friendship, despair and loneliness.
- Personification of objects (trees, ect) to add emotions and a sense of reality.

To summarise

By the end of this **Introduction Phase**, all the children should have experienced the text and have a basic understanding of its meaning. More confident and older children may also be able to read and/or recite the text with reasonable fluency. This means that cognitive space is not eaten up by struggling to decode or read sentences and, therefore, the brain can focus exclusively on comprehension and reading in a thoughtful way. As a result of this, children can often attain at much higher level than might be usually expected. In Talk for Reading schools, many children who might have struggled with comprehension benefit from splitting reading into two parts – basic 'reading' and 'comprehension'. This shift in focus allows them not only to grow in confidence with fluency in basic reading, but also to achieve a far higher level than expected with comprehension. With younger children, the weight of the actual reading is taken over by the teacher so that the children can focus on understanding the text. Teachers often ask how long this might take. There is no set rule, of course, as it depends on the text and the students. However, there naturally comes a point where the work begins to deepen and shift beyond understanding at a literal level.

Chapter 4: The Investigation Phase

Deepen understanding of the focus

Pie Corbett

By the end of the **Introduction Phase**, children should have read the text a number of times and have a basic understanding. This prepares them for the **Investigation Phase** where the text is studied at a deeper level. Generally, there is no specific move from one phase to another; you will find that you move naturally into deeper discussions.

The Investigation Phase

Deepen understanding of the focus through:

- oral comprehension;
- strategic reading;
- response activities;
- exploring structure and effect;
- summarising;
- evaluating;
- reading fluently.

This phase will help the children:

- deepen their understanding and enjoyment of the whole text;
- deepen understanding of any specific literary focus or key question/s.

Comprehension is what happens as we read, but can also be developed after we have read, through discussion. This may then enrich second, third or more re-readings of the text. Indeed, great books resonate in the mind and stay with us long after the actual reading has finished.

Talk for Reading lessons are characterised by a strong focus on responding to the text. This involves clarifying and refining our personal interpretation of it by digging deeply beneath the surface. You can select approaches described in this chapter and the order in which they might be used. **You do NOT have to cover every aspect**. What you do is determined by what the text needs to bring it alive, and what the children need to help them understand.

The main teaching approaches are described in the following pages. In some instances, it may make sense for you to thread the core literacy focus that you established at the end of the **Introduction Phase** throughout this phase of teaching. In others, it may work better if you attend to the literary focus towards the end of this phase. It will be dependent on the text you are investigating and your class. The teaching approach is a blend of dialogic reading and direct modelling, all based on the notion of the gradual release of responsibility from teacher to pupil. As previously stated, constant pausing when re-reading a text can be irritating, but also may make comprehension more demanding, especially for those with a weak short-term memory.

However, as the chosen text should be challenging, it is important to consider where to pause and think more deeply about a particular section. Where this happens is, of course, dictated by the text and the pinch points where comprehension may fall apart or need deepening.

This chapter focuses on these seven key aspects of the **Investigation Phase**:

1. Oral comprehension
    - Modelling being a reader
    - Thinking aloud like a reader
    - Dialogic talk
    - Bit-by-bit reading
    - Questioning
2. Strategic reading
3. Response activities
    - Drama and performance
    - The arts
    - Talking and writing in role
4. Exploring structure and effect
5. Summarising
6. Evaluating
7. Reading fluently

1. Oral comprehension

The prime strategy for Talk for Reading is to use discussion to develop understanding. This involves children teasing away at the meaning of a text and sharpening and shaping their ideas through a well-orchestrated discussion. One of the biggest challenges for teachers is that this approach demands putting to one side the idea that you are the sole possessor of comprehension, and all the children have to do is guess what is inside your head. The aim is to develop the habit of thinking critically and thoughtfully about what has been read. It recognises that we all interpret texts in the light of our own experience, and therefore, there will be shades of meaning to share. Explorations of the text should start with talking about what the text meant to us, to our past, present and future and who we are as human beings. This can arise naturally by discussing simple things, such as what we liked or did not like about the text.

These sessions are about the children's comprehension. The initial skill is to get the class sharing ideas, listening to each other and developing their thinking. This can be a challenge as many classes can be unused to actually having anyone interested in their thinking! In terms of comprehension, the old model of constant testing is still prevalent – either you know the answer, or you do not. For those who are uncertain, this practice just reinforces the idea that reading is something they are not good at, and this becomes a self-fulfilling prophecy.

Within oral comprehension, there are five core strategies that form part of the approach.

- **Modelling being a reader** – the teacher being a role-model for reading.
- **Thinking aloud like a reader** – the teacher demonstrating what should be happening inside children's heads as they read.
- **Dialogic talk** – talking about the text together to reach a shared understanding.
- **Bit-by-bit reading** – slowing the reading down and tying together the clues.
- **Questioning** – raising queries that need exploration.

Modelling being a reader

With younger children in the EYFS, modelling being a reader will include aspects such as book handling, turning pages carefully one by one and scanning from left to right. You might also be modelling using book language, such as *front/back cover*, *page*, *word*, *sentence*, *glossary*, *chapter*, *page numbers*, etc. The objectives of the sessions will relate to the children's specific needs as developing readers.

It is also essential that we reflect on the importance of being strong role models for children, reading with fluency and expression, exuding passion for literature, and modelling how to be effective, critical and appreciative readers.

Thinking aloud like a reader

Thinking aloud like a reader involves you revealing what is happening in your head as you read. It's rather like giving a running commentary and is often known as doing a 'think aloud'. It works in the same way as during shared writing when you might talk aloud like a writer about the decisions being made to make the thought processes of being a writer obvious. In reading, a 'think aloud' may end up with a mix of predictions, questions, statements, connections, mini summaries, what you can see in your head, talking about how characters might feel, links to your life, describing how it makes you feel or think, ideas about vocabulary meaning, and so on. There are three ways to use this strategy, which are described on the next page.

i. Revealing in general what is happening as we read in our heads:

> *"OK, so there's an Iron Man at the top of the cliff. I can see him standing there – we don't know yet, but I suspect that the Iron Man will not be a good character. It sounds a bit dangerous standing at the edge of the cliff. I wonder what he is doing. I'll read on a bit... So, no one knows where he came from or how he got there. He sounds a bit lonely standing there..."*

A potential difficulty with this approach is that there may be too much going on and less confident children may become confused.

ii. Focusing on one aspect of reading

This is very useful, especially where there is some aspect of reading that you feel needs further modelling or explication, e.g. tying ideas together across a passage by linking pronouns or using inference to build a picture where things that happen are not explicitly stated:

> *Jon picked up the lemon and ate it in one gulp. Mrs Parton watched as he spat it out.*

> **Teacher modelling:** *"Now we have been thinking about making sure we tie everything up from line to line. So, we have a boy called Jon who has just eaten a lemon. Lemons are sour so that won't have tasted very nice. I wonder what he does. In the next sentence, we have a new character called Mrs Parton. She could be his mum. She is watching him. That word 'he' means Jon. I know that because she is watching him, and he spits it out. That means Jon is spitting out the lemon because it was sour. So, Jon is 'he' and the lemon is 'it'. OK, let's re-read the whole thing now."*

iii. Focusing on a core literacy concept

It is useful to model core concepts, such as focusing on how a character feels:

> *Victor trudged along, silently. At the end of the lane, he gripped his school bag tightly and increased his pace, glancing all around.*

Teacher modelling: *"Right, I'm thinking about the main character, Victor, and trying to work out how he might be feeling. He is 'trudging' and that means walking slowly and heavily – it makes it sound as if he is weary or reluctant. The author also adds that he is going 'silently' and I'm wondering why he might be 'silent'. Perhaps he doesn't want anyone to hear him for some reason. In the next section, he grips his bag 'tightly' – is he afraid he might drop it, or someone might grab it? He's now speeding up and glancing around. It sounds as if he has reached a place where he thinks he might need to walk more quickly and warily, looking around. I think that he may be afraid of being attacked, perhaps by bullies so he didn't want to reach that point in his journey, but now he is there, he's going faster in case he gets attacked. I'll need to read on to see if I am correct... but before that, I'll re-read to see if I am right so far."*

Read a passage and show the class how to underline the key words and phrases that suggest how the character is feeling. Then talk through why you have chosen the words or phrases you have, and what they are conveying to you as a reader. You might then work on an example together, before letting the class loose, independently or in pairs, on an extract such as this:

Grandpa adjusted his tie, nodded to himself in the mirror and grinned. He patted his wallet, winked at his reflection and stepped outside to a cheering crowd.

You can use this method to go through a core section of the text, bit-by-bit. Listen carefully to the children's 'think alouds' so that you can respond helpfully, especially remembering that texts do not mean any old thing so you may have to model 'referring back to the text'.

Watch out, too, for children who make what Jane Oakhill calls 'wild inferences'. This is where a child comes up with an idea that is vaguely within the realms of possibility, but it is very unlikely, given what we know about life, how books work and the evidence in the text. Take the class back to the text to come up with possibilities and then consider 'what is most likely'. For example, in this text:

Jose sulked as they sped along. She knew that they would soon arrive at the station. She gripped her ticket tightly as she would be in trouble if she lost it.

Using this snippet, I once had a child suggest that Jose is in a bad mood about travelling in a rocket to a space station on Mars! Of course, this *could* be possible, but the more likely scenario is that she is being taken to a railway station and is reluctant for some reason.

Dialogic talk

Dialogic talk is, in essence, a class or group involved in dialogue around the reading. There are a few key points that underpin these sessions.

- **All ideas are accepted** – this doesn't mean that children can say any old thing or that all ideas are going to be insightful. What it does mean is that everyone's ideas will be listened to, valued and taken seriously.
- **Everyone should 'have a go'** – teachers often find that a 'no hands up' approach helps as everyone is expected to be thinking, joining in and ready to share their ideas, even if they are not yet well formed.
- **Be ready to change your mind** – this is key because the aim of the discussion is to grow our understanding through sharing different ways of looking at the text and justifying suggestions.
- **Listen to each other** – essential in all discussions and often shown by children referring to what someone else has said.
- **It helps to be tentative**, e.g. *"We wondered whether..."*. Framing comments in this way can be useful as it puts less pressure on the speaker to be 'right'. It is worth collecting useful sentence openers such as, *"I'm wondering whether..."*, *"I'm not sure, but perhaps..."*.

Good discussions centre more on the children doing the thinking than the teacher. Your role is to encourage deep thinking through being a good listener, keeping the conversation going, re-phrasing for clarity, repeating ideas, holding up thoughts for further consideration, returning to the text, giving mini summaries, challenging ideas and encouraging different views and justification. To an observer, it may appear that you are not doing much. However, to run a good session you have to be thinking on your feet and know the text really well. Questions or statements from you help to open up thinking, as well as pinpointing aspects that may be essential but have been glossed over. To that end, a mix of very open questions should be used, plus those that encourage further exploration, and the occasional closed question to help scaffold the understanding. If you are ready to learn alongside the class, it makes it easier as the questions become increasingly genuine rather than 'test based'. A key skill involves leading the conversation on from what someone has just said, and this cannot be planned for.

- *Can someone clarify what Sue is saying...?*
- *Can I check that I have understood...?*
- *Is there a different way to look at this...?*
- *What do you think Sue means by saying...?*
- *Can anyone explain why this line/page/point matters...?*

Take time and don't be afraid to leave pauses for thinking. If I am ever uncertain about what to do next, I throw it back to the class with, *"Have a quick chat in pairs about this."* This gives you time to regroup and almost inevitably some of the class will have more to say. For the children, it is not the occasion to blurt out the first thing that comes into their head! Gradually, they learn to think more critically.

Training children in a few basic notions helps the discussions become more fruitful. You might find it useful to introduce them to these sentence starters for framing their thoughts and opinions.

- **Suggest a new idea** – *I think... because...*
- **Challenge** – *I'd like to challenge Jenny...*
- **Build on an idea** – *I'd like to build on Raj's idea...*
- **Explain ideas** – *Can Kabir explain further why he thinks...? I think I can explain why...*
- **Question** – *We were wondering why... I'd like to ask if anyone has any ideas about what/why/how/when/where/whether...*
- **Justify** – *The author states... I think that... because it states that...*

See **Handouts 1 & 2 (online)** for further examples of sentence stems and oral comprehension guides.

It is worth displaying and using any relevant key vocabulary to help with discussion and comprehension, as illustrated in this image from a flipchart.

Put a poster up in the classroom with useful words and phrases, such as:

characterisation
compare
contrast
flashback
foreshadowing
metaphor
symbolise
viewpoint
pivotal moment
zoom in

The more often children hear us use technical language, the more likely they will be to feel confident using it themselves.

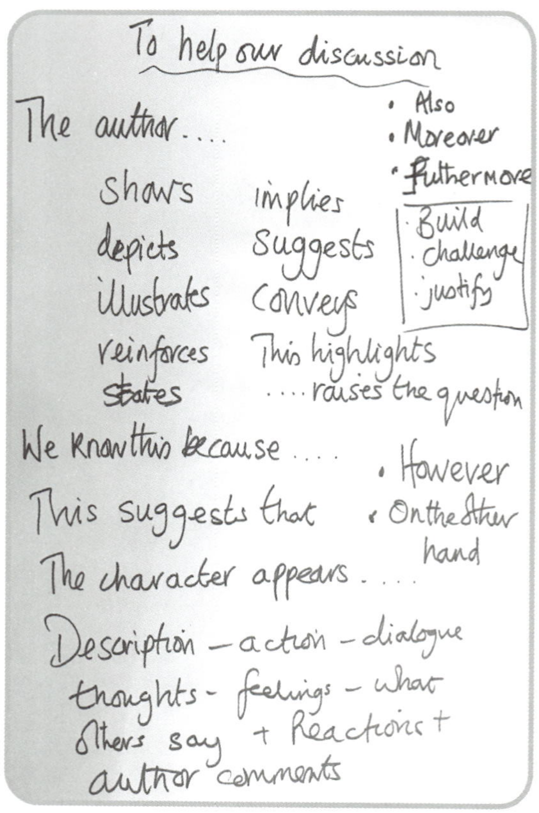

Intersperse the discussions by using mini whiteboards for children to write down their thoughts or craft a reply to a comment. Reading journals (or 'magpie' books) are essential at KS2 so that children can be constantly jotting down notes, juicy quotes, etc. This means that they are not forgetting what has been said and can capture ideas.

The extracts below are from Isadora's 'magpie' book and show her notes during a discussion about 'viewpoint' in Anthony Browne's *Voices in the Park*. The transcript follows this.

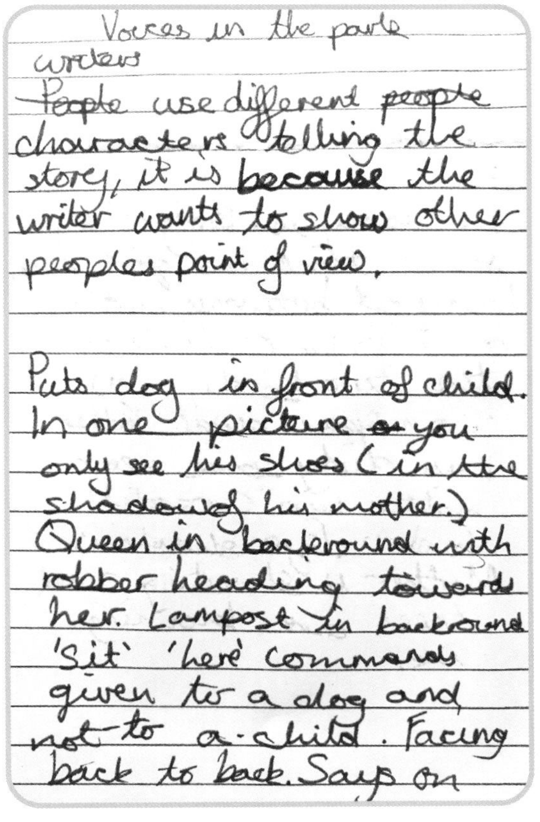
Voices in the park
writers
People use different people characters telling the story, it is because the writer wants to show other peoples point of view.

Puts dog in front of child. In one picture you only see his shoes (in the shadow of his mother.) Queen in background with robber heading towards her. Lampost in backround 'Sit' 'here' commands given to a dog and not to a child. Facing back to back. Says on

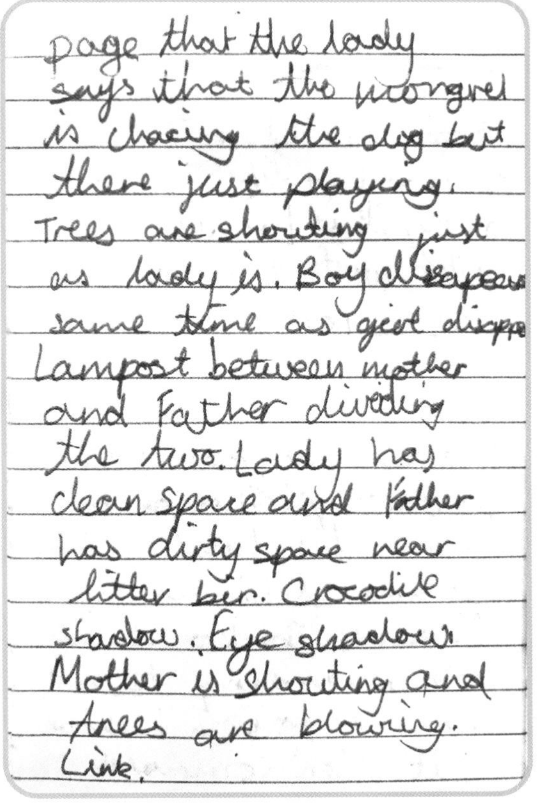
page that the lady says that the mongrel is chasing the dog but there just playing. Trees are shouting just as lady is. Boy disappears same time as girl disapp Lampost between mother and Father dividing the two. Lady has clean space and Father has dirty space near litter bin. Crocodile shadow. Eye shadow. Mother is shouting and trees are blowing. Link.

Voices in the Park

Writers use different characters telling the story, it is because the writer wants to show other people's point of view.

Puts dog in front of child. In one picture you only see his shoes (in the shadow of his mother). Queen in background with robber heading towards her. Lamppost in background. 'Sit', 'here' commands given to a dog and not to a child. Facing back-to-back. Says on page that the lady says that the mongrel is chasing the dog, but they are just playing. Trees are shouting as lady is. Boy disappears same time as girl disappears. Lamppost between mother and father dividing the two. Lady has clean space and father has dirty space near litter bin. Crocodile shadow. Eye shadow. Mother is shouting and trees are blowing. Link.

If the conversation lags, then bring it to a close with a summary as it can always be returned to in another session, perhaps taking a different tack or with an activity. The summary could be made by you or as a five-minute, short-burst writing activity.

Here is an extract from a Year 5 'magpie' book, summarising a page from *Voices in the Park*, following the discussion. Again, a transcript of the notes has also been included:

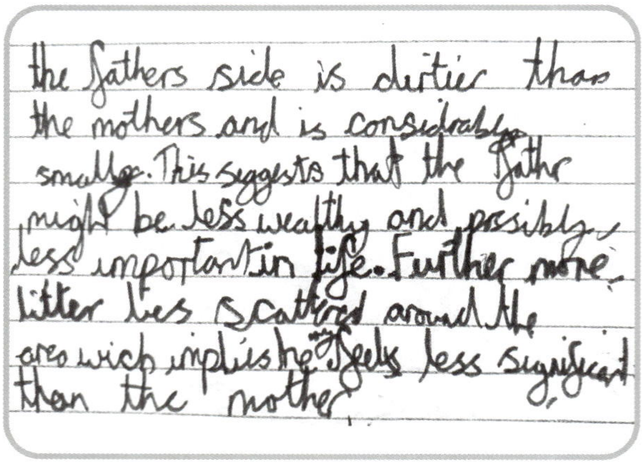
the fathers side is dirtier than the mothers and is considerably smaller. This suggests that the father might be less wealthy and possibly less important in life. Further more, litter lies scattered around the area wich implies he feels less significant than the mother.

The father's side is dirtier than the mother's and is considerably smaller. This suggests that the father might be less wealthy and possibly less important in life. Furthermore, litter lies scattered around the area, which implies he feels less significant than the mother.

Whilst dialogic talk is taking place, children are speculating, refining and developing lines of thought and constantly clarifying their reading. In complex texts, this may well involve linking ideas, views, scenes or information together through constantly summarising to build a global picture of the text. When we get this right, lessons sound rather like a serious conversation in an adult book club. To this end, the study of literature allows us to take part in a conversation enriched by our past experience. It is a dialogue where we learn together from drawing on our perceptions of the text, blended with what we have been formally taught and our life experiences. Great texts stay with us, add to our inner lives and the discussions around them can change ideas. This is why books get burned and authors imprisoned. The word is powerful.

Dialogic reading is a collective endeavour, and the atmosphere has to be one of trust where no one feels that what they have to say will not be accepted and listened to with serious consideration. Fear or a sense of *'I cannot do this'* has no place. Ideas should be shared, different readings appreciated, and you should be as interested as the children in everyone's thoughts.

Aidan Chambers, in his seminal work, *Tell Me* (Thimble Press), developed what he called 'booktalk' and this is well worth reading. *Tell Me* is a 'master class' in using dialogue to develop understanding. However, the term 'booktalk' has become widely misappropriated to mean any old discussion where we talk about books. We use the term as a child-friendly phrase to describe dialogic reading.

For those new to dialogic reading at KS2, it can help to cut your teeth on a picture book, such as *Voices in the Park* by Anthony Browne as the book is rich with possibility, illustrated by **video clips 5 & 6**, where I am leading a class discussion. It is also worth looking at **Chapter 8** for a worked example using this book. One advantage of picture books for teaching comprehension is that everyone can 'read' the pictures. Often the actual words in picture books are easy enough to read, but the book may be hard to understand. In **video clips 7 & 8**, Jamie demonstrates dialogic reading in both Year 2 and Year 6.

Bit-by-bit reading

Often known as 'close study', bit-by-bit reading involves slowing the text down so that children get into the habit of considering shades of meaning and making connections between sentences and across a text. A key aim is to support the development of the working memory. The children should be trained to read bit-by-bit, tying ideas together and clarifying meaning as they go along. This has the effect of them revising their thinking in the light of new information. Develop this skill so that it ultimately becomes a habit of reading, where children notice if meaning is falling apart and are confident enough to re-read more carefully.

On these flipchart extracts below, you can see that the children were reading as a class, bit-by-bit, through a section of Shakespeare's *Macbeth* and focusing on the changes in the main character's mood.

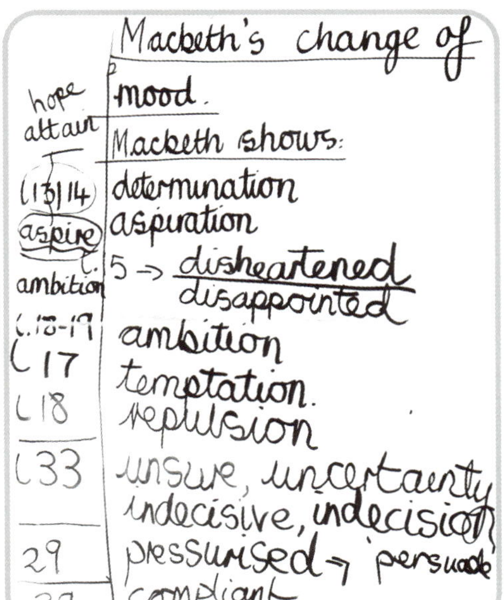

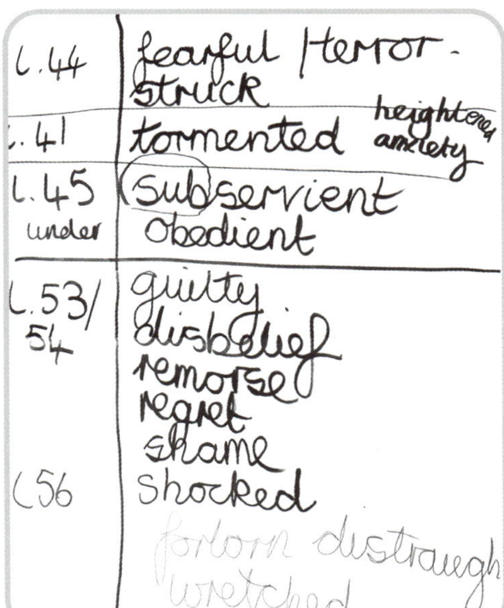

Through gradual scaffolding and building on each other's thoughts, and sometimes challenging them, the class can discuss and co-construct new thinking which deepens understanding. When this is done well, you will find your own understanding grows with new insights gathered from the children.

In the following extract, it is perfectly possible to have children who can read and know the meaning of every word, but still not understand what has happened across the text.

Gary ran down the road, clutching the enormous goldfish bowl. Rain swept across the town and already the streetlights were flickering into life. He ran faster. A moment later, there was a terrible noise and glass scattered across the road. Within minutes, a policeman was comforting the boy who sobbed bitterly. The present was ruined!

There are two issues here. The first is to do with the way in which the text is tied together. *'Gary'*, *'He'* and *'the boy'* are all the same person. The space between mentioning *'Gary'* and *'the boy'* might well lead a child into thinking that this was a different boy who was crying. Another connection involves realising that the *'goldfish bowl'* links to the *'glass'* and *'The present'*. In this instance, the author is using different nouns to name the same thing which can be confusing. The connecting phrases (*'A moment later'* and *'Within minutes'*) help tie events together. The second issue is to do with the way in which writers often don't state explicitly what is happening and leave the reader to fill the gaps. So, we are not told that Gary has fallen over and have to infer this from the fact that *"A moment later there was a terrible noise and glass was scattered across the road."*

Bit-by-bit reading can be used to help children make these connections:

Teacher modelling: *"OK, so Gary is running – I wonder why he is running – perhaps he is late? Let's read on, 'clutching the enormous goldfish bowl'. OK so, he's running along and 'clutching' – that means holding tightly – a goldfish bowl – and we know they are made of glass. It doesn't sound very sensible – what might happen? Mmm, so the next bit tells us that it is raining, and the lights are coming on so it's getting dark. So, we have Gary, holding tightly onto a glass bowl and running even faster as it is getting dark, and the pavements are wet. Do you think that's sensible? I wonder what might happen... Oh dear, there's a terrible noise and there is glass everywhere – what has happened to Gary and the goldfish bowl? Yes, it sounds like he's fallen over and smashed the bowl. That must have hurt..."*

Video clip 9 shows me demonstrating bit-by-bit reading with a simplified version of this text – this time relating to a girl called Polly.

Jane Oakhill suggests that there is a significant percentage of children in each class who can read at a reasonable rate and know what the words mean, but find it hard to tie the ideas together. The issue is usually about making inferential links between sentences and across the text. In these instances:

- model as suggested on the previous page to support children in making more efficient use of their working memory;
- provide children who find it hard to remember things plenty of practice as the problem is related to fact recall;
- use shorter extracts, as with longer texts the process will take too long, and the immediate links may become lost;
- use text marking or circling to show the links;
- pause and ask for summaries, *"let's think about/make a note of what we know so far"*;
- use re-reading to strengthen and make obvious links between sentences, considering how a sentence links back to something that's just been read;
- ensure constant 'comprehension monitoring' and clarifying.

Video clip 10 shows me exploring the first paragraph of a short story (included below) with a Year 4 class.

Poppy had always been curious. One sunny afternoon, she was walking down Elf Road when she saw something unusual. In the brick wall, there was an ancient, wooden door. The metal handle was shaped like a dragon's mouth. Gently, she turned it and the door creaked open.

I begin by asking about the main character and receive a very literal retelling. Without making it obvious, I then take the children through the paragraph bit-by-bit, pinpointing the key pinch points so that understanding builds. In terms of her character, a key word is 'gently' because it suggests that whilst she is curious, she also realises that it might be dangerous to open the door. I end the video by asking about her character again, having read the paragraph more carefully.

Questioning

Good questions take us back into a text, to think deeply. Weak questions lead away from the text or have obvious answers. In many KS2 classes, pupils make notes or discussions are recorded by the teaching assistant on the flipchart and used as a basis for shared and independent writing. A 'questioning' session involves you having a variety of carefully thought through questions about a text – **closed**, **explorative** and **open**. Let the children brainstorm a list of their own questions and then select which ones to discuss. Do not worry if the conversation veers into new avenues, as long as they seem fruitful.

Questions can focus on summarising the **whole** text, but also dig into 'what the text is about' and invite discussions on the overall themes or messages.
They might also focus on clarifying particularly **tricky sections**. They could invite speculation and the whole business of wrangling with meaning and clarity.

Some of these sessions will also have the sort of questions that are part of the national testing regime, especially selected to be pertinent to gaining deeper understanding. Careful discussion of the questions, where to look in the text and how to frame replies are all part of useful preparation for exams. It is not fair on children to dodge sensible preparation. High attaining schools do this, but it does not dominate as a main approach. Following a discussion about the ways in which Macbeth's hands are "hangman's hands" and exploring the phrase "filthy witness", Jessie in Year 6 writes:

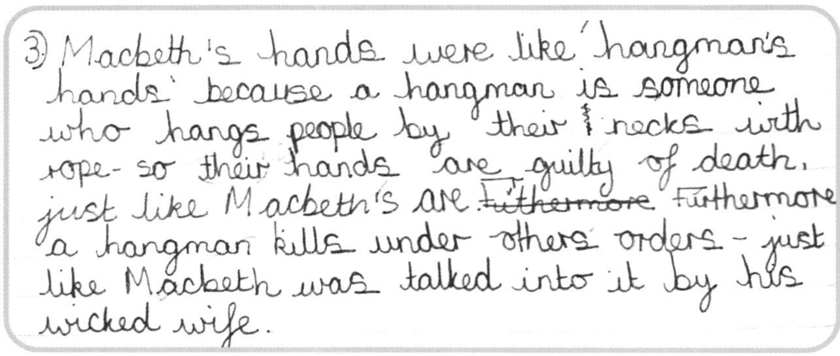

3) Macbeth's hands were like 'hangman's hands' because a hangman is someone who hangs people by their necks with rope- so their hands are guilty of death, just like Macbeth's are. ~~Futhermore~~ Futhermore a hangman kills under others orders - just like Macbeth was talked into it by his wicked wife.

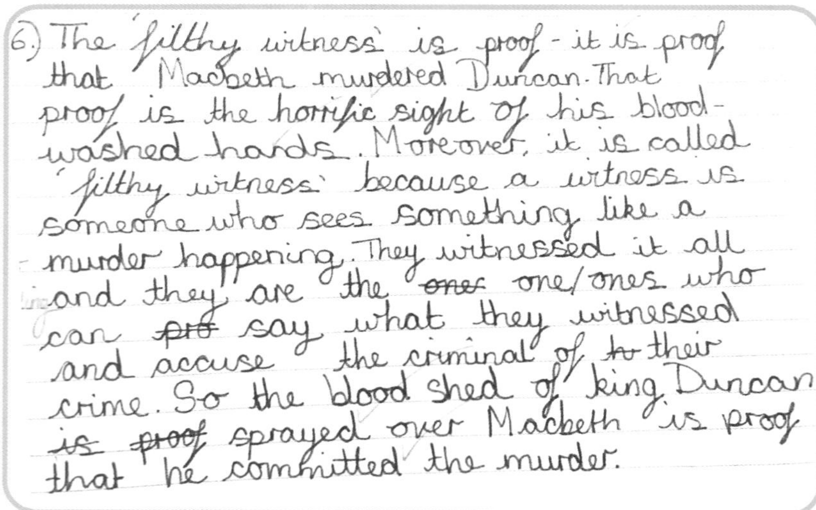

6.) The 'filthy witness' is proof - it is proof that Macbeth murdered Duncan. That proof is the horrific sight of his blood-washed hands. Moreover, it is called 'filthy witness' because a witness is someone who sees something like a murder happening. They witnessed it all and they are the ~~ones~~ one/ones who can ~~pro~~ say what they witnessed and accuse the criminal of ~~to~~ their crime. So the blood shed of king Duncan ~~is proof~~ sprayed over Macbeth is proof that he committed the murder.

We have seen many rich sessions where the teacher has created a sharp focus on a thematic or stylistic element of the text and, through shared discussion, modelled how to respond discursively or critically to the text. This can be where we explore how any specific elements contribute to the overall purpose of the text. Here are some question ideas to do this:

Role of characters/issues/information:
How does the character's emotional journey through the text link to the core theme of sacrifice?

Role of setting/mood/tone:
How does the author use the setting to create the atmosphere, i.e. how does the setting make you feel as a reader?

Structure of text – how the text works:
Why has the author decided to start the text with a prologue? How does this affect you as a reader?

Use of language, including figurative language:
How has the author's language choice throughout the text influenced your understanding of the key themes that lie at its heart? (See the example here.)

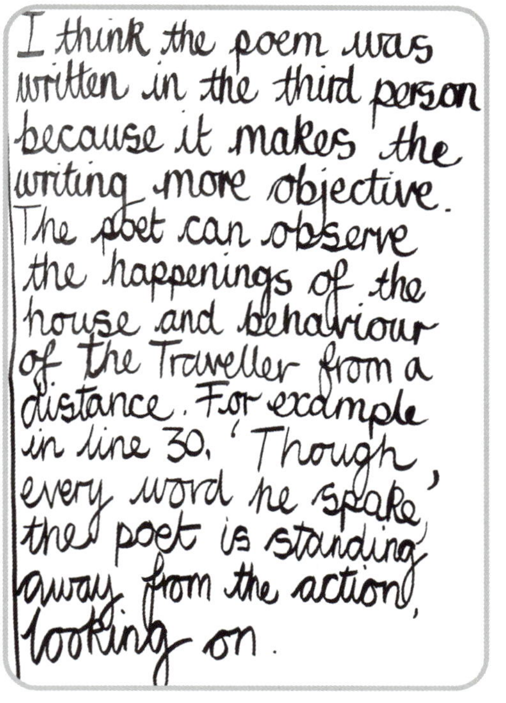
I think the poem was written in the third person because it makes the writing more objective. The poet can observe the happenings of the house and behaviour of the Traveller from a distance. For example in line 30, 'Though every word he spake' the poet is standing away from the action, looking on.

Writer's perspective
What is your impression of the author's stance on the key theme or subject explored in this text?

Reader's viewpoint:
What are the different views about the nature of heroism? Which is expressed most powerfully. Which do you agree with and why?

See **page 16** for more information on the initial brainstorm around literacy concepts. **Handout 5 (online)** provides banks of question stems/styles to support planning and teaching (linked to the assessment domains in England).

2. Strategic reading

Where the children are engaged in reading a challenging text, inevitably there may well come a point where they get stuck and need to read strategically. It's worth holding explicit discussions about what would help or what strategy could be used. Core strategic approaches include:

- **Self-monitoring** – noticing when we don't understand.
- **Slowing it down** – noticing when a section might be tricky so slowing the reading down to make the required effort to concentrate, clarify and tie ideas together. It is worthwhile to then re-read that section and check that we have understood.
- **Re-reading** – realising that we need to read again slowly and carefully. It can help to take notes, highlight sections, jot down mini summaries or underlying key ideas.

- **Finding the main ideas** – as with re-reading, it can help to make notes on the core ideas or scenes across a text. It's useful to create sub-headings or even use drawings to track what is happening and then putting it all together. In these images, you can see the child has used a grid to extract core information about Colin and Mary's characters in *The Secret Garden* by Frances Hodgson Burnett, which then leads into more extended writing:

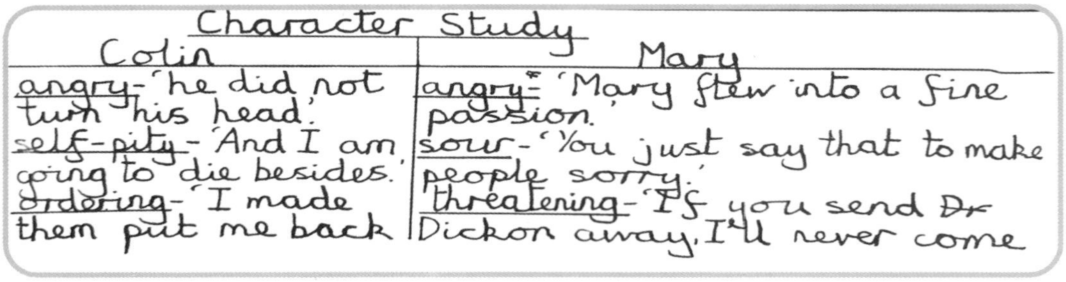

Character Study

Colin	Mary
angry- 'he did not turn his head.'	angry- 'Mary flew into a fine passion.'
self-pity- 'And I am going to die besides.'	sour- 'You just say that to make people sorry.'
ordering- 'I made them put me back	threatening- 'If you send Dickon away, I'll never come

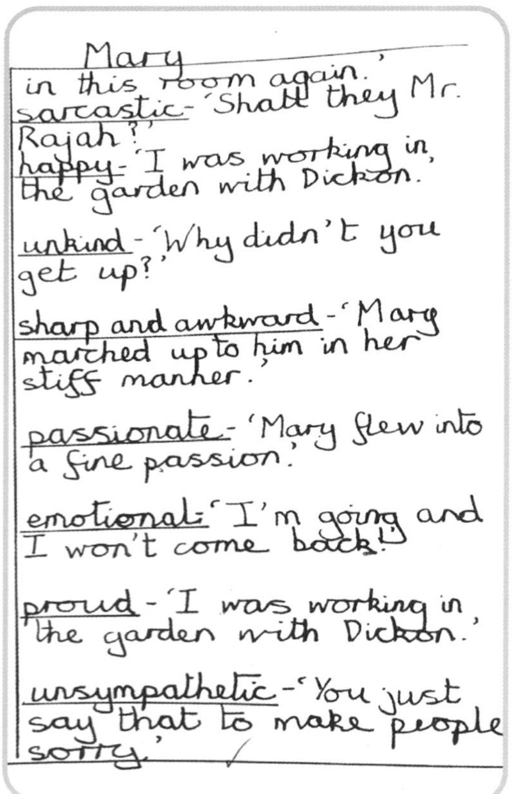

Mary

in this room again.'
sarcastic- 'Shall they Mr. Rajah?'
happy- 'I was working in the garden with Dickon.'
unkind- 'Why didn't you get up?'
sharp and awkward- 'Mary marched up to him in her stiff manner.'
passionate- 'Mary flew into a fine passion.'
emotional- 'I'm going and I won't come back!'
proud- 'I was working in the garden with Dickon.'
unsympathetic- 'You just say that to make people sorry.'

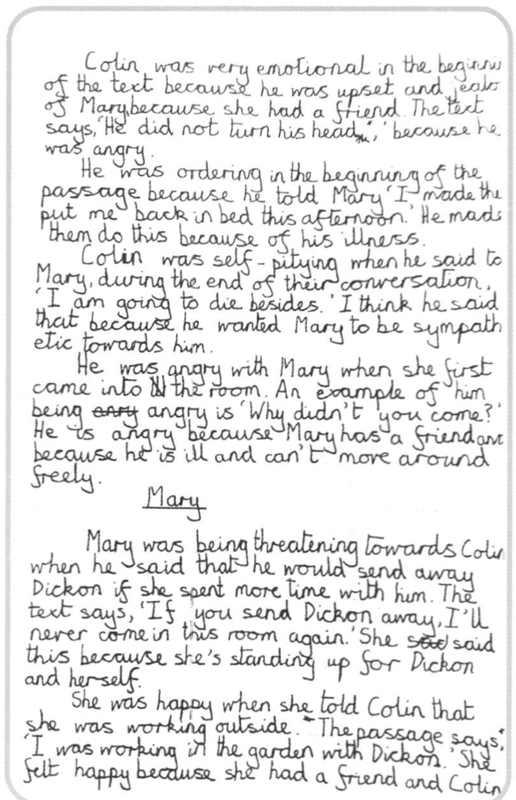

Colin was very emotional in the beginning of the text because he was upset and jealous of Mary because she had a friend. The text says, 'He did not turn his head,' because he was angry.

He was ordering in the beginning of the passage because he told Mary 'I made the put me back in bed this afternoon.' He made them do this because of his illness.

Colin was self-pitying when he said to Mary, during the end of their conversation, 'I am going to die besides.' I think he said that because he wanted Mary to be sympathetic towards him.

He was angry with Mary when she first came into the room. An example of him being angry is 'Why didn't you come?' He is angry because Mary has a friend and because he is ill and can't move around freely.

Mary

Mary was being threatening towards Colin when he said that he would send away Dickon if she spent more time with him. The text says, 'If you send Dickon away, I'll never come in this room again.' She said this because she's standing up for Dickon and herself.

She was happy when she told Colin that she was working outside. The passage says, 'I was working in the garden with Dickon.' She felt happy because she had a friend and Colin

- **Paraphrasing and summarising** – these strategies are handy with complex texts to avoid getting to the end and not being able to create that global picture.
- **Graphic representations** – Talk for Writing has long used the strategy of mapping texts. The beauty of this approach is that the reader can see the whole plot or structure in one glance. *Tom's Midnight Garden* by Philippa Pearce shifts about, so creating a timeline can be helpful when thinking about the structure. Boxing-up texts into a flowchart is also a very useful tactic for seeing how a short story or non-fiction text is organised.

- **Non-fiction** – **skimming** needs to be taught to help children get the gist of a text. **Scanning** helps to locate specifics (though also learning to use **chapters** and **subheadings**, as well as **indexes** are key skills). Children also need to be aware of the need to consider when we are being spun an **opinion** and identifying what is a fact. **Video clip 11** shows Tracey Adams using a challenging non-fiction text on heroism in Year 6.

More about non-fiction can be found in **Chapter 7**.

3. Response activities

Our main strategies for deepening response are:

- **Drama and performance**
- **The arts**
- **Talking and writing in role**

The more we work deeply with texts and the arts, the bigger the memorable 'living library' grows inside every child.

The focus of response activities is to help children make connections from their own lives with the text, forming a personal relationship with it so that it means something to them. It is also about devising activities that help them inhabit the world of the text so that they experience it at a much deeper and more emotional level. This involves explicitly setting out to develop the ability to imagine – taking what we know and manipulating that to engage more deeply.

Whilst it is important for children to have books read to them for the sheer enjoyment of the experience, this can be enhanced through well-chosen activities. If we dramatise a story, dance an event, or create music to accompany a character's emotions, then we may enter into the story at a deeper level, taking us closer to its heart. For a moment, we become the story.

A word of warning – we can all take a book and think of 30 different things to do (*"let's paint the cover"*, *"let's make a model fox"*, etc.). The skill is to decide which parts of a story would benefit from an extra activity, putting key events under an imaginative lens for closer consideration. Select important moments and pause for deeper exploration. In this way, the children's experience of the story slows down so that events are not glossed over in rapid, superficial reading.

Drama and performance

This helps the class explore a text collaboratively through a range of emotional, dramatic responses in order to develop a greater empathy for characters, themes, ideas and situations. In a case where children may struggle to have an emotional connection and reaction to the text, consider how you can help them relate to the characters and begin to see things through their emotions and feelings. Choose or invent a drama activity linked to a desired purpose. Some schools use 'one minute drama' – these are mini-interludes in lessons where there is a brief drama activity. Where teachers and children are not used to drama, we have found these work better than trying to hold a whole session using drama. Here are some ideas you could try with your class.

- **Freeze Frame** – choose an important specific moment in a story and ask groups to create a tableau of the scene. Interview the characters in the tableau or get them to reveal what they are thinking.
- **Eyewitness, on-looker or spy** – invite volunteers to retell what has happened as if they are an eyewitness to a key incident in a story or a real event from a non-fiction text. This helps to develop perspective.
- **Rumours about the main character** – ask children to take it in turns to act in role as the main character so that they can explore the character's back story and perspective, or even thoughts about what might happen next.
- **Jump into a scene** – this enables children to explore what they see, hear, feel and think as if they are the main character in a key scene of the story. It helps them to build empathy and deepen their connection with the character. For non-fiction, they could 'jump into an event' and speak as a witness.
- **Speaking picture** – *I am the...* children could become the setting, a character or a key object in the story. This enables them to visualise an important moment or develop empathy for a character.
- **Hot-seat a character** – another useful activity to develop empathy and understand a character's emotions and motivations.
- **Conscience alley** – in this activity, children can get into the character's mindset, tune into the author's voice and interaction with the character, and explore the emotions of the character.
- **Professor 'know-it-all'** – in role as experts, children could present ideas and information from the text.
- **Role-play** – children could act out the scene after the book has finished or before the story starts. Alternatively, select an image from the middle of a picture book and discuss what is happening. Children could then role-play what might have happened before or after this. Children could also act out an event that doesn't happen in the story, but is referred to by the writer.
- **Gossip** – organise the class into pairs and ask them to chat about the events that have happened to deepen their understanding of the plot and structure.

- **Agony aunt** – this is useful for stories where the characters have problems to solve. Put the children into pairs, where one child plays the role of the troubled character and shares their worries, and the other child is in role as an agony aunt and gives advice.
- **Phone calls** – similar to 'Agony aunt' above, the pairs sit back-to-back, and the main character explains what is going on to their friend on the phone who responds with advice.
- **Word and gesture** – choose a favourite word or line from the text and get everyone to stand in a circle. The children then take it in turns to step into the circle, say the word aloud with a gesture and everyone else copies this.
- **Mime and actions** – as above with 'Word and gesture', but this time you choose an action from an event in the text that is memorable. Children then take it in turns to mime the action and everyone else imitates this.
- **Actions and grammar** – select all the verbs from an action passage and list them in the order that they appear. As a class, say them aloud with expression. Discuss with the children what effect this has. Now try the same thing with adjectives or nouns from an extract. This powerfully demonstrates the importance of word choice.
- **In role as journalists** – you play the role of a character while the children interview you for a written or filmed news item.
- **Hold a trial** – put especially bad characters on trial. One child could be the baddie and the rest of the class could be the jury. (I once saw this done in Year 4, where the jury took a long time to decide whether the troll was guilty or not as the defendant claimed to have been threatened by the goats with sharpened horns!). This is useful to understand motive and explore character traits.
- **Retell** – in pairs, children can retell the text word-by-word or sentence-by-sentence.
- **Group performance** – in the hall or outside, read the story to the children while they act it out freely.

Drama helps children re-experience and enter the story imaginatively, becoming characters or witnesses to the events. It emotionally engages them with the writing in a way that pure reading might not touch.

Handout 3 (online) provides practical ideas for using drama to work with the picture book *I'll take you to Mrs Cole* by Nigel Gray and Michael Foreman.

The arts

Deepening engagement and understanding can also be developed through the arts – music, singing, dance and visual art. Again, it is easy to overload a unit of work with artistic activities that are fun to do and pass the time of day, but do not necessarily focus sufficiently on any objective. *How might the arts add to children's understanding of the text itself and any core focus?* The key is to think about what activity will illuminate the meaning of the book, help children engage at a deeper level and enter the world of the text. Here are some activities that might trigger your imagination when planning.

- **Drawing, painting and model-making** – this helps children visualise scenes and characters. They could Illustrate sections of a story, turn a chapter or a poem like *The Highwayman* by Alfred Noyes into a cartoon to track events, draw the map of the story, create a mural or diorama or design a front cover.
- **Dance** – help children to emotionally engage with events or characters by creating a dance together. You might choreograph a dance to fit the section when Skellig and the children move together or dance to the 'rumpus' in *Where the Wild Things Are* by Maurice Sendak.
- **Percussion and mood music** – a useful way to help children interpret atmospheres in a potentially more memorable fashion, e.g. performing *We're Going on a Bear Hunt* by Michael Rosen with percussion and actions. Many early stories have songs that accompany them, such as *When Goldilocks came to the house of three bears*. Lots of Julia Donaldson's stories can also be sung and acted out.
- **Build a story museum** – represent the novel, poem or picture book by gathering and displaying objects, sounds (use *Talking Tins*) and images from the story.

Talking and writing-in-role

Encouraging children to take on the role of a character in a story is a powerful way to focus the mind on different viewpoints, as well as themes, ideas, information or situations. We have found that writing-in-role works best when following on from drama, so that the children have had time to experiment and play with being the character. Like the drama and art activities, the children should read the text closely to extract the relevant details. You could explore a range of spoken and written responses with the children, including ideas from this list (below and on the next page), drawing on their suitability. Revisit models to remind everyone of the relevant structure and style, and use shared writing to create a bridge into their independent writing.

- **Diary extracts** – children could retell core events in role as different characters, e.g. the Brightstorm twins' diary entries about leaving on their adventure, producing a contrast of views (*Brightstorm: A Sky-Ship Adventure* by Vashti Hardy).

- **Letters or postcards home** – challenge the class to have a go at writing these from various characters or between characters, e.g. Goldilocks apologising to the bears, or one character offering another character advice.
- **Interviews** – children might enjoy acting as roving reporters and interviewing key characters and witnesses in the story, who can respond in role about what they saw or heard.
- **Newspapers** – why not get children to write short news reports about key events, including interviews with characters from the story? For example, they could write about the death of Smaug in *The Hobbit* by J. R. R. Tolkien.
- **News bulletins** – children could write and record a news bulletin using either audio or film, e.g. reporting about a bomb raid in *Letters from the Lighthouse* by Emma Carroll.
- **Discursive article for a magazine** – writing in this style enables children to explore issues, viewpoints or factual reports, e.g. summarising Greta Thunberg's views.
- **A poetical response** – this involves children responding to a text by writing a poem, e.g. they could write a list poem called 'I wish' after reading *The Three Wishes*.
- **Re-write a section** – when doing this, children could change elements such as the main character or setting. Alternatively, they might like to write the events in a different text type, e.g. the ending of *Little Red Riding Hood* as a news report. They could also explore 'what if' events to change the plot and deepen understanding of a character, e.g. what if Podkin gave up? (*The Five Realms Series* by Kieran Larwood.)
- **Write the next part** – why not challenge children to continue a text in the same style as the author and use prediction to guide the content? For example, start Chapter One of *Malamander* by Thomas Taylor, following the prologue.
- **Creating documents from the text** – this might include story maps, messages, charters, etc. that are referenced in a text, e.g. writing entries for Butterwick's Guide to Better Manners, when reading *Cogheart* by Peter Bunzl.
- **Promoting the book** – children could write the back cover blurb or an advert about the book to encourage people to buy it.
- **A 'for sale' advert** – what about exploring the positive traits of a character with a snappy strapline?
- **End of term report** – this is similar to the 'for sale' advert activity, but this time children should also include the character's weaknesses as well as their strengths.

The following examples show Year 6 children from Penn Wood Primary School writing in role as the different characters in Anthony Browne's *Voices in the Park*. This response activity supported the children's understanding of viewpoint and perspective which are core literary concepts in the story.

Voices in the park

The lamposts are shaped as a hat. Furthermore, there is a broken plane which represents that Charles might fall and hurt himself. As well (as), the reflection on Charles is like the Scream in the newspapper. Secondly, the slide gets bigger to make it like it's coming out of the page.

Why?

Third Voice

The lampost have hats on like Charles's mother, well she always has a hat on! Also, the snowdrops suggest that it's spring with all the blossom and flowers as well as, blue sky which represents hopefultness.

Further more the dogs are having a fun time chasing each other around, and I think Charles and Smudge maybye starting to have quite a fun time. Moreover there's a broken plane on the floor, which hints that Charles might fall and suggests he's scared. Also, with the look on his face he might feel the slide's too high. Additionally, the slides almost coming out of the page with a 3D offect which makes the page more exciting, by enlarging the action.

The shifting shadows play over the grass as the clouds speed by. As well, it's bright and cold I can see the reflection of Charles on the slide it looks like The Scream in the newspaper that Smudge's dad has. You can tell how cold it is because Charles is wearing long trousers, gloves and a coat done up right to the top. Because its cold no one is sitting on the benches and they normally would on a sunny day.

The whole park looks so clean and tidy, the trees are in neat rows, the grass is cut short and the flowers form an orderly line I cant see any rubbish or litter, perhaps its all in the bin at the top of the hill. As well as that how new the slide is, with no rusty parts on. More over, thestruts of the slide have shadows coming off them, perhaps it is late afternoon, because the sun is low to make shadows.

It might be worth saying how untidy some of the other scenes were.

Although Charles clearly looks very worried Smudge is just the oppisite, even though she is standing on the highest part of the slide she still looks confident and eager to have a go, she doesnt need a coat or gloves, unlike Charles. The picture of Charles looks stiff and wooden whereas Smudge on the otherhand has more movement in her. to show her self-confidence and carefree personality.

Why do you think this is?

The playground has been designed thoughtfully, because it is really well covered with bark chipping, this means it will be soft and springy iff anybody falls over. Also it will be grippy under foot. Whereas, the grass would get muddy and wet, but the bark chippings would keep your feet clean and dry.

It's noticable that Charles and Smudge are the only characters on the page so your attention is automatically drawn to them. Also, theres no birds but usally there is especially in a park that is really quite. Maybe because Anthony Browne wants us to just focus on Charles and Smudge and their friendship.

Wonderful homework.

You have noticed so much, Maddie and so much that is important in the picture. Always try to add why you think the artist has drawn things in the way he has.

4. Exploring structure and effect

Exploring structure and effect encourages the reader to step back and consider the writing objectively as an artefact. This form of reading involves looking at any underlying patterns in the text, the author's word choice, the manipulation of syntax, and use of literary concepts like imagery. It is training children to think about how the writing creates an effect on the audience, linked to the writer's purpose.

Structure

Understanding how a text is structured helps to build essential understanding. If we know that an information text is likely to have an index, then we know that we don't have to read through the whole text to find information.

Christopher Booker in his book *The Seven Basic Plots*, identifies different common plot lines: *"Overcoming the monster, Rags to riches, Quest, There and back again, Tragedy, Rebirth and Comedy"*. Many short stories and picture books lend themselves to children drawing the story map and moving on to drawing a story mountain, graph or flowchart that shows the key scenes. This helps to unpick the plot pattern, so children gain a sense of story architecture and are able to discuss dilemma, resolution and how suspense might be built over time.

It is important to introduce the concept of the different sections to a story early on (opening, build-up, problem, resolution and ending). In the EYFS, you could start with discussions of the **beginning**, **middle** and **ending** of a story. Story maps and mountains can clearly show the pattern and these discussions equip children with the simple, but vital language, and understanding to talk about story structure.

Story type	Example	Pattern
Quests and journeys	*The Hobbit* by J. R. R. Tolkien *Little Red Riding Hood* *Where the Wild Things Are* by Maurice Sendak *Rosie's Walk* by Pat Hutchins	A character travels in search of something or someone – or to find something or someone. Either from A to B or there and back again.
Cumulative tales	*There was an Old Woman who Swallowed a Fly* *The Very Hungry Caterpillar* by Eric Carle *The Enormous Turnip* *On Friday Something Funny Happened* by John Prater	Very strong repetitive pattern where an initial action or event is built upon. Each time a new action or event is added, all the previous ones are repeated.
Warning stories	*The Minpins* by Roald Dahl *Why The Whales Came* by Michael Morpurgo	The main character is warned not to do something or go somewhere. They ignore the warning and get into trouble.
Overcoming the monster	*The Iron Man* by Ted Hughes *Jack and the Beanstalk* *The Wooden Horse of Troy*	Everything is fine until a threat appears. Eventually this is overcome.
Wishing tales	*The Three Wishes* *Galactic Snapshots* by Kenneth Oppel *The Fib* by George Layton	A story involving someone who wishes for something, but usually there is a barrier that has to be overcome. A variation of this story type would be about a character who is granted a wish but wastes it.
Transformations	*Cinderella* *The Gift from Winklesea* by Helen Cresswell *Woof* by Allan Ahlberg *Beauty and the Beast* *The Snow Goose* by Paul Gallico *Harry Potter* by J. K. Rowling *James and the Giant Peach* by Roald Dahl	A character is transformed in some way – rags to riches, ugly to beautiful, timid to brave. Occasionally, the transformation involves changing 'form' or personality. In some stories a character learns so much that their views or feelings are transformed.

Story type	Example	Pattern
Losing and finding	*Owl Babies* by Martin Waddell *Charlotte's Web* by E. B. White *Little Red Hen*	A character finds or loses something of value.
Rescues	*Sleeping Beauty* *The Magician's Nephew (The Chronicles of Narnia)* by C. S. Lewis	A character has to be rescued.
Meeting someone	*E.T. the Extra-terrestrial* written by Melissa Mathison and film directed by Steven Spielberg *The Dancing Bear* by Michael Morpurgo *The Butterfly Lion* by Michael Morpurgo *The Midnight Fox* by Betsy Byars	The main character meets someone or something that then leads to a dilemma, such as the person or thing having to be looked after or kept secret.
Character flaw	*My Naughty Little Sister* by Dorothy Edwards *Horrid Henry* by Francesca Simon	The main character is basically sympathetic but has a flaw, e.g. is greedy or does something silly.

The more that children and teachers look at stories, the easier it becomes to identify the fundamental story pattern (or blend of patterns). To do it, you have to stand outside the detailed meaning and try to notice the underlying structure, reducing a story down to its main elements. Once these have been drawn as a story map, grid or flowchart, the children can visually see the main sections and how the text is constructed.

Effect

Analysing the writing for effect requires the reader to pause, step back from the immersive experience of the book or text and consider the writer's intent. This might include how they hook us in, create suspense, immerse us in a believable setting, craft characters that we love or hate, inject pace through action, leave us longing for more, etc. To enter into these discussions, it helps to ask the children:

- *What effect is the writer creating in this passage?*
- *How have they created this effect?*

To begin to unpick the techniques or 'tools' the author has used, you will need to begin with close reading. This may draw upon dialogic techniques, such as bit-by-bit reading.

For instance, in this short extract, *how is the writer building the suspense?*

> *Joanne stood alone in the dark and listened. She could hear something scratching...*

There are at least six key techniques that the author uses:

- The character is alone.
- The character is in a dark place.
- The character can hear something making a noise.
- We are not told what is making the noise. The word 'something' hides whatever it is so that the reader's imagination kicks in.
- The alliteration (sibilance) in 'something scratching' creates a snake like hiss.
- The idea of 'scratching' suggests a creature or something desperate to escape.

By extracting these simple ideas from the text, we now have what we refer to as a as a 'toolkit' for writing. These tools can be applied to a new piece of suspense writing, as illustrated below.

> *Mrs Bonny paused at the end of the car park. It was quite dark and the car park was empty. At that moment, she heard a noise. Something or somebody was standing by her car...*

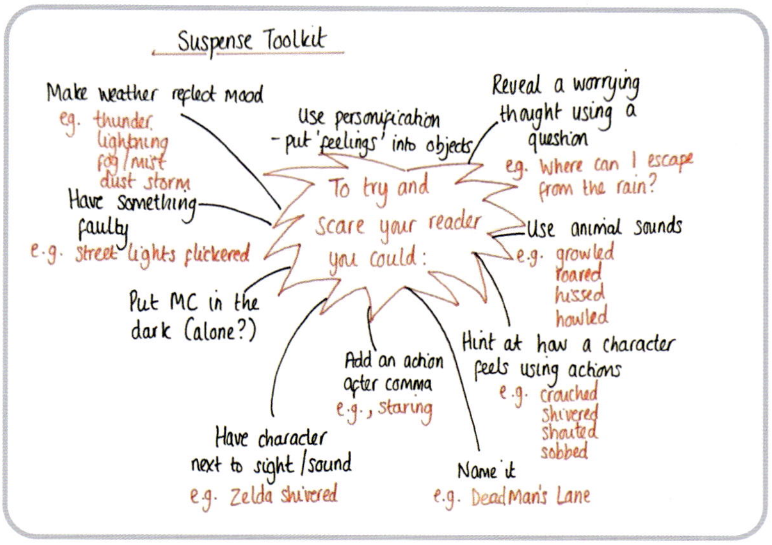

This toolkit was co-constructed with a Year 4 class at Warren Road Primary, Orpington. The text was explored bit-by-bit so that the children had time to talk about the effect the writing had on them before discussing how the author created it. **Video clip 12** shows this bit of teaching in action.

Being able to talk about how the writer is creating a desired effect on the reader is an important part of building comprehension. You can use this to enhance general understanding or any specific focus or question. You may be working with word choice, a sentence or a paragraph.

- *What is the purpose of this part?*
- *How did the writer create…?*
- *Which words make you feel…?*
- *Why did the writer choose to use the word/phrase… rather than…?*
- *Can you find the words that make us feel frightened/sad/happy?*
- *Why do you think the author used/included…?*
- *What is the intention of this sentence?*
- *What's the most important word/sentence/paragraph?*
- *What was the main dilemma/problem?*

5. Summarising

Increasingly, we have come to believe that summarising is central to reading proficiency. If you cannot summarise as you read, then the text is just words on the page. Have you ever had that experience when reading of getting to the bottom of the page, but not remembering a thing? Your reading mind was not sufficiently pulling the threads together and creating a whole schema for what was happening in the text. To read efficiently, the brain has to be constantly summarising what has happened and then tweaking, adjusting and refining this as new information arrives.

Summarising involves pausing at key points and pulling the threads together before moving on to another stopping point to, once again, pull the threads together. Underlining key ideas, making notes in the margin, creating little subtitles, turning the text into a flowchart of main scenes or ideas are all useful strategies for helping children navigate through a challenging text.

It also entails pulling the whole thing together and shifting from the particular into the general. *What is this story or poem about? What is the main thrust of this article?* Children often get lost in the particular and less confident readers may find it hard to step back from the text and think about the overall meaning.

It is helpful if, from the very start in the early years, we hold discussions about themes and big ideas that capture the essence of a text. Initially, this will need to be modelled. However, as children grow in experience of doing this, one useful stepping stone towards independence is to provide them with a range of statements and challenge them to choose which one captures what the text is about best.

Children can summarise:

- what happened in a story;
- the main ideas;
- core information;
- the theme/s;
- a line of argument;
- a character's motives;
- the core dilemma and resolution;
- what a character learned;
- how characters change;
- how a setting influenced a story;
- how the word choice influenced the reader;
- how the symbolism worked in a poem or story;
- how rhythm and imagery created an effect on the reader.

It is important to remember that the summary is gathering all of the learning together across the unit and reflecting on the core focus that you have been investigating with the children. It is not looking for simple retrieval statements, such as *"Little Red Riding Hood's cloak was red"*, or *"There were three pigs in the story."* In fact, *The Three Little Pigs* is not really about pigs, nor is it about building houses. So what are the children actually learning?

- *What were the key scenes in the story? (What happened between the pigs and the wolf?)*
- *What are the main ideas that the story explores? (Friendship, teamwork, trust, problem solving, planning and bullying.)*
- *Why did the wolf try to blow down the houses? (Character motivation.)*
- *What did the first two pigs learn? What did the wolf learn? (Lessons being learned through the story – possible morals.)*
- *How were the different setting in the story important? (Setting influencing the plot.)*
- *How do we feel about the characters in the story? Did this change at any point? (The overall effect on the reader.)*

Video clip 13 shows Tracey Adams teaching Year 6 children to summarise as part of a guided reading session.

6. Evaluating

Evaluation is linked to summary because to evaluate you have to reflect on the big picture of the text in some form. Mature readers are evaluating as they read. *Is this worth persisting with? Is this a line of argument I want to stay with? Are these facts relevant to my interests? Can I really devote time to a novel with paper-thin characters?* As we read, we are forming an opinion about the text and its value.

A tricky aspect for children is that they have to have grown a sense of what the whole text has done for them, making generalisations. Younger children find this hard and will often try to retell the particulars. A simple starting point is to discuss preferences – likes and dislikes, and what the text means to different individuals. By Year 6, children should have a bigger frame of reference and be able to judge a book against others with a sense of appreciation. Discussions can shift to talking about which book is better or more effective and why. In this way, children build up a sense of themselves as a reader in terms of the sorts of books and authors that they enjoy reading. Good books may also introduce children to new ideas, challenge their own perceptions so that they think differently.

- *Did you enjoy the text?*
- *What was it about the text that held your attention?*
- *Why did this text mean a lot to you?*
- *What has stayed with you from this text?*
- *Did your views on the text change over the time we worked with it?*
- *In what ways has this book been successful?*
- *What did you learn?*
- *Have your views changed?*
- *Are there other books like this that are better – why?*
- *Explain in what ways this book is better?*
- *Who would benefit/enjoy this book and why?*
- *Was there information that was not needed?*

Class discussion usually leads to children writing about what they have appreciated in a text as well as critically discussing the strengths and weaknesses of the text.

Below you can see a pupil's response to Anthony Browne's *Gorilla*, following class discussions about what can be learned from looking carefully at the illustrations.

It looks as if Hannah surrounds herself with comforting objects. She seems to be having a private conversation with her toy gorilla, possibly to reassure herself. The bed appears very large and she appears very small. Also, the colourful bed cover and floral wallpaper indicate that she has some hope.

When the gorilla appears in Hannah's room that night, Hannah's bed suddenly looks very small while the gorilla seems to fill the room, dominating the scene.

This example below from a KS2 boy who felt that he wasn't a writer, shows the power of the approach. He wrote this following a class discussion and shared writing about an image in Shaun Tan's *The Arrival*.

Faces filled with sadness, sorrow and tear-stained.
Ornaments staring, ticking, falling apart.
The room cold, damp, narrow, old and broken.
Touching, memories fading, gentle, loved.

As I touched my son's trembling hand, my eyes immediately turned from love to sorrow. My eyes filled with tears; warm water came trembling down my face and dropped silently onto my hand. I thought this was the last time I would be having a cup of tea with my son. Sadness continued to creep over me. The clock finally struck 12 o'clock, time to leave. We bid goodbye and farewell.

7. Reading fluently – the final performance

By the end of this phase, where the children have been digging deeper into the text, a key aim for older children is that they should be able to re-read it independently with accuracy, effortlessly, at a reasonable pace, and with understanding and expression. In other words, with fluency. For younger children, the actual text may be too far from their ability to decode. With re-reading, they are likely to join in with memorable aspects, though this is memory rather than actual reading.

This is focused very much on what might be described as 'performance reading'. When I taught, we called it 'BBC reading'! You model how a reader hears a text in their head and explicitly teach children how to connect with intonation and expression to convey understanding. This could be a poetry choral performance or presenting an information text or story in sections by different groups. No one should be pressurised into reading solo if they do not feel sufficiently confident. However, the aim is to develop confidence so that everyone is happy to take part. The main reason why children do not want to read aloud is a lack of confidence, and through being asked to read aloud without preparation and modelling. We recommend the following steps to help eliminate the fear of performance:

- You read the text or an extract without expression and children discuss why this does not work and how the expression should sound.
- You read each sentence with expression (sometimes exaggeratedly), changing the volume, pitch or tone of your voice.
- Children follow and text mark to indicate your performance (e.g. where you pause/slow down/change volume, tone or pitch, etc.)
- You re-read bit by bit with children copying your tone and intonation.
- You invite groups, trios, pairs and individuals to prepare sections for 'performance reading'. This is where the children read aloud with expression. Provide sensitive feedback to help them to improve.
- Finally, children end with a performance of the text, reading it without your support. You could make this a regular feature in assemblies. It could be filmed and played back for further consideration.

Video clip 14 shows Jamie Thomas developing fluency with a Year 2 class to demonstrate how intonation promotes understanding.

In **video clip 15**, you can see a wonderful performance of Tennyson's *The Charge of the Light Brigade* set to music by Year 4 children from Selby Community Primary School. As you watch, you can tell by the way the children are performing that they understand the meaning of the text. They have mapped, orally learned the text and had meaningful discussions about it, which has led to their comprehension.

Chapter 5: The Independent Understanding Phase

Demonstrate levels of understanding

Pie Corbett

The Talk for Reading approach enables children, through shared and guided practice, to develop themselves as thoughtful and strategic readers. It teaches them how to read and make sense of high-quality texts and, ultimately, understand themselves and the world around them. This third, **Independent Understanding Phase**, provides the opportunity for them to demonstrate understanding independently.

The Independent Understanding Phase

Demonstrate understanding through:

- talking or writing as a reader about the core text; or
- identifying the key focus in another text and responding; or
- applying what they have learned in their own writing.

In **Chapter 4**, we considered how, by the end of the **Investigation Phase**, the children should be able to read the selected text/s confidently and fluently, with understanding and expression. They will have spent time thinking more deeply and critically about the text, exploring and clarifying its meaning. They will have considered any big questions and developed understanding of any key literary concepts. By now, most of the active comprehension has happened during the reading, discussion and linked activities. This prepares the children for this final phase.

Enabling children to demonstrate what has been learned

Across a Talk for Reading unit, children should move from dependence towards independence. To enable the children to demonstrate what they have learned, discuss and reflect on any transferable literary concepts or strategic aspects of reading that have been used across the **Investigation Phase**. There is sufficient reading research to suggest that making these explicit links helps children apply their learning to future texts.

When planning opportunities for children to demonstrate what they have learned across the unit of work, it is important to reflect on the unit synopsis that you drew up in **Chapter 2**. The purpose of this synopsis was to focus your teaching on the transferable elements of learning – the elements that we are now encouraging children to apply. Demonstrating understanding might involve the children writing extended discursive pieces, exploring a focus through dialogic talk or applying their knowledge of the focus to similar texts. It may entail exploring and answering a 'big question', such as: *Explain how, in the final paragraph, the author reveals their own viewpoint about climate change*. The important point is that children are provided with a suitable text in order to demonstrate how they have developed as a reader across the unit of work.

When considering independent understanding, we may ask ourselves:

- *Can children demonstrate understanding through talking or writing as a reader about the core text?*
- *Can children demonstrate understanding through identifying the key focus in another text and responding?*
- *Can children demonstrate understanding through applying what they have learned in their own writing?*

Demonstrate understanding of the core text through talking or writing as a reader

At the heart of Talk for Reading is rich discussion and exploration of a high-quality text. Through the dialogic approach to reading, there will be many 'lightbulb moments' where concepts or themes are realised and identified with clarity and supportive evidence. It is not always easy to capture these moments, but independent understanding does not always have to be demonstrated through a written response.

Teaching reading requires you to notice how a child thinks both critically and emotionally. Just as understanding in maths can be acquired through discussion, practise and application, so too can understanding in reading. Ensuring that there is quality debate and discussion around texts will often provide ample opportunity for children to demonstrate understanding. With younger children, you may observe their understanding of the core text through responses during class, guided or one-to-one discussions.

When faced with a challenging text, there is also the opportunity for children to independently demonstrate understanding using a strategic approach that has been modelled to them. This can often be through a written response, focusing on a key strand, such as the role or development of characters in a text.

The following example on the next page demonstrates how a Year 4 child has learned to consider contrasting characters, picking up on clues in the text that reveal how a character thinks, feels or behaves. Having read an excerpt from Peter Bunzl's *Cogheart* as their Talk for Reading text, and explored several characters, they were then given a subsequent passage to respond to. In this written response, the child shows their understanding of how to write a critical piece, supporting their opinion with evidence and explanation. It is a first draft on a mini whiteboard. The transcript is also set out below.

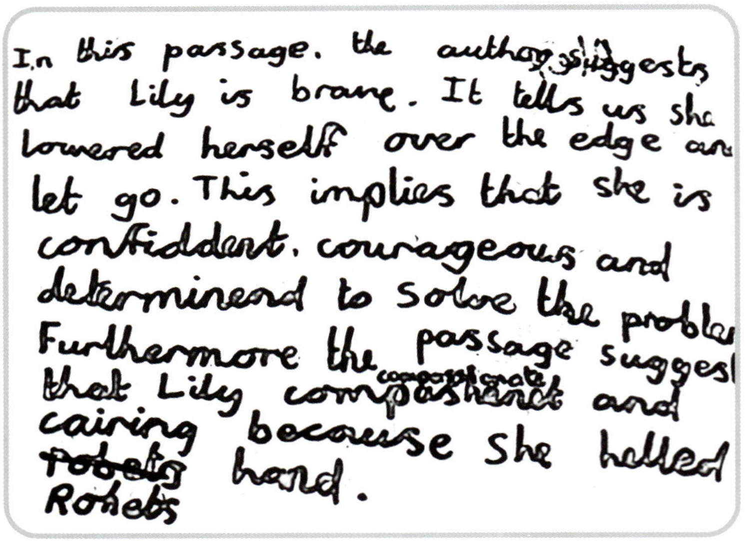
In this passage. the author suggests that Lily is brave. It tells us she lowered herself over the edge an let go. This implies that she is confiddent. courageous and determinerd to solve the proble Furthermore the passage suggest that Lily compassionate and cairing because she helled Robets hand.

In this passage, the author suggests that Lily is brave. It tells us she lowered herself over the edge and let go. This implies she is confident, courageous and determined to solve the problem. Furthermore, the passage suggests that Lily is compassionate and caring because she held Robert's hand.

Video clip 16 shows me co-constructing with a class how to write effective answers.

In the child's writing, pictured below, there is an extended character study based on Chapter 8 from *A Pack of Lies* by Geraldine McCaughrean. This is presented as a transcript on the next page.

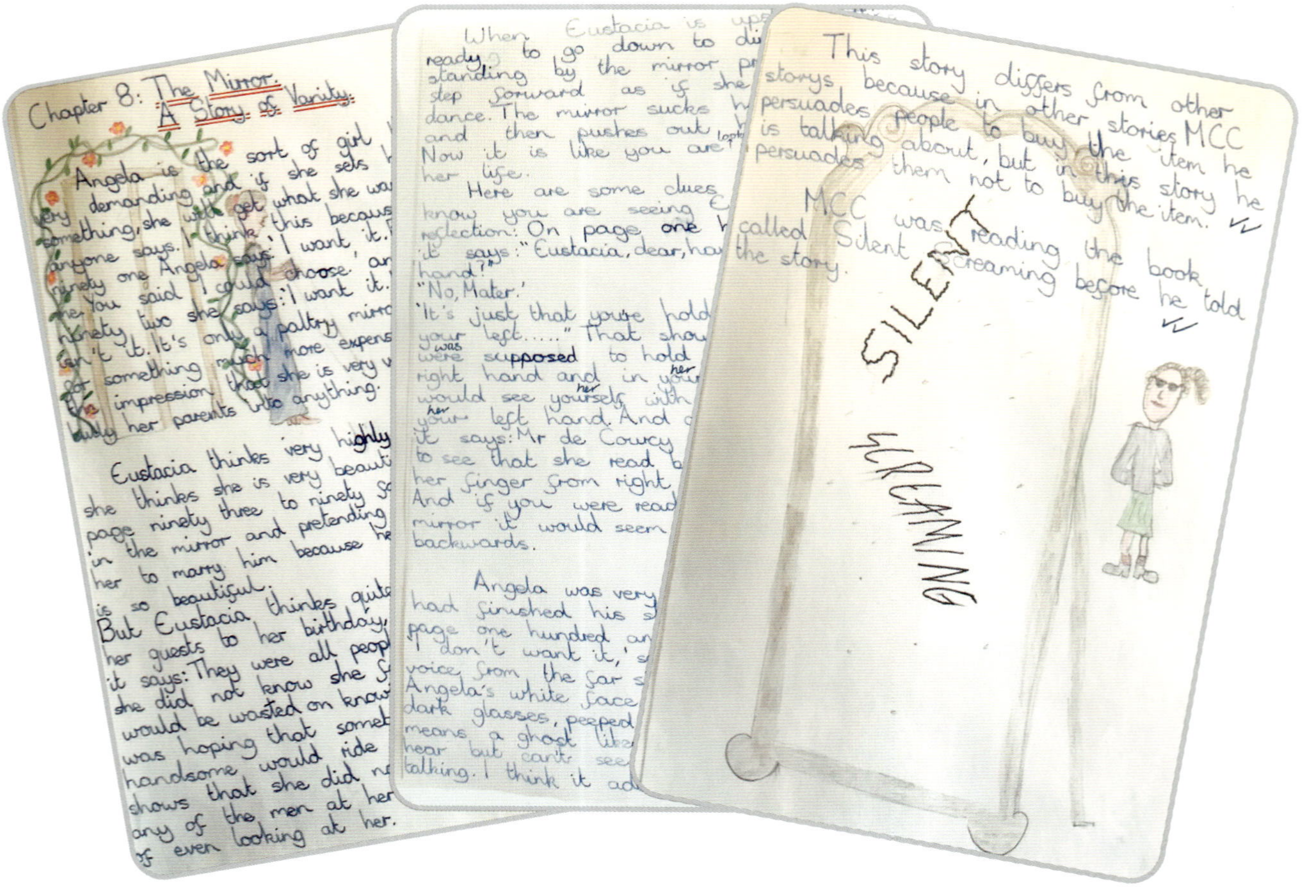

Chapter 8 The Mirror: A story of Vanity

Angela is the sort of girl that is very demanding and if she sets her mind to something, she will get what she wants, whatever anyone says. I think this because on page ninety-one Angela says: "I want it. Buy it for me. You said I could choose" and on page ninety-two she says: "I want it. It's my birthday isn't it? It's only a paltry mirror. I could ask for something much more expensive." And I get the impression that she is very vain and can bully her parents into anything.

Eustacia thinks very highly of herself. I know she thinks she is very beautiful because on page ninety-three to ninety-four she is looking in the mirror and pretending someone is asking her to marry him because he thinks that she is so beautiful.

But Eustacia thinks quite the opposite of her guests to her birthday, on page ninety-five it says: 'they were all people she knew and those she did not she felt that five minutes would be wasted on knowing them.' And Eustacia was hoping that somebody charming and handsome would ride in after them. This shows that she did not think that any of the men at her birthday were worthy of looking at her.

When Eustacia is upstairs, getting ready to go down to dinner, she is standing by the mirror pretending to step forward as if she was going to dance. The mirror sucks her into it and then pushes out her reflection. Now it is like you are looking in a mirror at her life.

Here are some clues about how I know you are seeing Eustacia's reflection: On page one hundred and one it says: "Eustacia dear, have you hurt your hand?"

"No Mater."

"It's just that you're holding your spoon in your left..." That shows us she was supposed to hold her spoon in her right hand and in her reflection you would see her with her spoon in her left hand. And on the same page it says: "Mr de Courcy was rather disconcerted to see that she read backwards. Running her finger from right to left over the text." And if you were reading in front of a mirror it would seem you were reading backwards.

Angela was very frightened when MCC had finished his story because on page one hundred and three it says: '"I don't want it," said a disembodied voice from the far side of the bed, and Angela's white face, blindfolded with the dark glasses, peeped into view.' Disembodied means a ghost like voice which you can hear but can't see the person who's talking. I think it adds to what Angela is feeling.

The story differs from other stories because in other stories MCC persuades people to buy the item he is talking about, but in this story he persuades them not to buy the item. MCC was reading the book called 'Silent Screaming' before he told the story.

The images below are from the flipchart of a Year 4 class, where the teacher is showing the children how to answer more traditional questions, based on the poem *The Listeners* by Walter de la Mare.

We can see clearly how the teacher is working with the class to craft answers, training them to:

- read the question carefully;
- make a relevant point supported by evidence from the text.

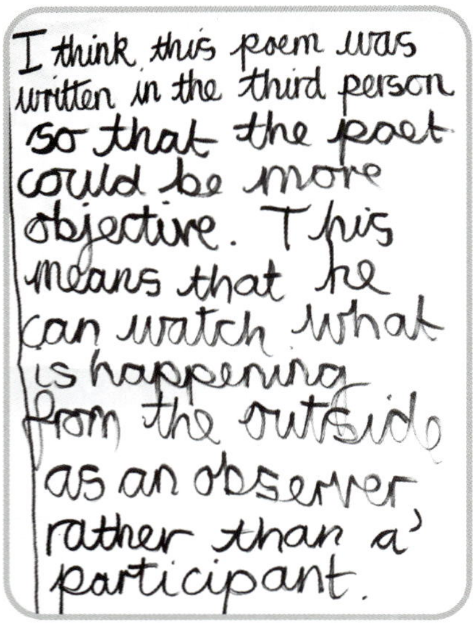
I think this poem was written in the third person so that the poet could be more objective. This means that he can watch what is happening from the outside as an observer rather than a participant.

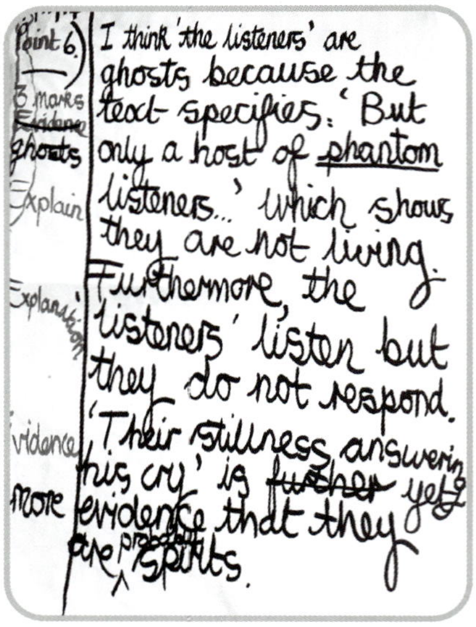

I think 'the listeners' are ghosts because the text specifies: 'But only a host of phantom listeners...' which shows they are not living. Furthermore, the 'listeners' listen but they do not respond. 'Their stillness answering his cry' is ~~further~~ yet more evidence that they are spirits.

The impact of such teaching can be seen in the children's independently written answers to a set of questions, based on the poem, that they then had to complete:

Child A's questions:

- *What makes the poem seem ominous? Find evidence from the text.*
- *Do you believe 'the listeners' are real? Use examples from the poem to support your answer.*

Child A's response:

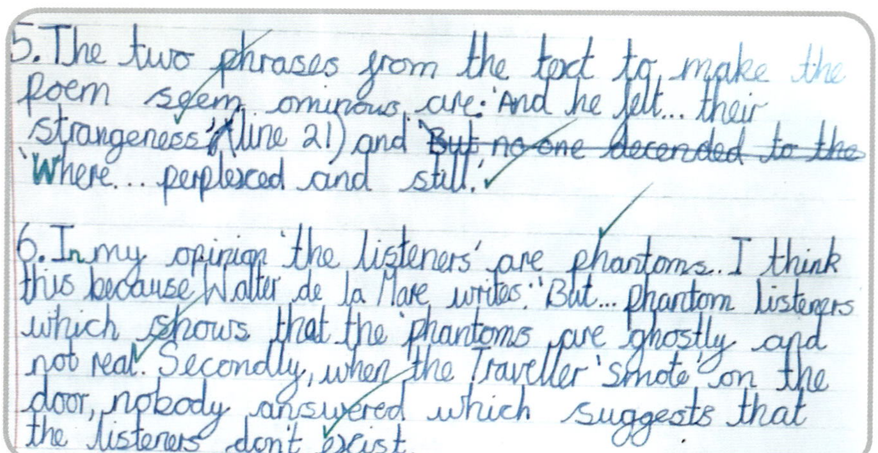
5. The two phrases from the text to make the poem seem ominous are: 'And he felt... their strangeness' (line 21) and ~~But no one decended to the~~ 'Where... perplexed and still.' ✓

6. In my opinion 'the listeners' are phantoms. I think this because Walter de la Mare writes: 'But... phantom listeners' which shows that the 'phantoms' are 'ghostly' and not real. Secondly, when the 'Traveller' 'smote' on the door, nobody answered which suggests that the 'listeners' don't exist.

Child B's questions:

- *What impression of the traveller is the poet trying to make on the reader? Use the poem to show evidence of this.*
- *What atmosphere does the poet create in the poem? Give examples from the poem.*
- *What makes the poem seem ominous? Find evidence from the text.*
- *Do you believe 'the listeners' are real? Use examples from the poem to support your answer.*

Child B's response:

I think the impression that the poet makes of the traveller is that he is brave, hence the words: 'And he felt in his heart their strangeness' (Line 21) which shows that he knows how strange they are but he was brave enough to stay and knock again. Secondley, I think he is also impatient as it shows in the phrase: 'For he suddenly smote (hit hard) on the door,' (Line 25) which shows us he cannot wait for an answer.

4b) Walter de la Mare suggests a gloomy ~~ap~~ atmosphere by using words like: 'dark' and 'shadowiness'. He also uses the word 'moonlight' which suggests a dark and gloomy atmosphere apart from the moonlight. In adittion, he uses the phrase: 'Leaned over... his grey eyes.' Which suggests it is so gloomy you can't see their real colour.

The two phrases that make the poem feel ominous are: 'But no one descended to the traveller' and 'And he felt in his heart their strangeness.' (Line 21).

In my opinion 'the listeners' are phantom. I think this because Walter de la Mare writes 'But... phantom listeners' which shows that the 'phantoms' are ghostly and not real. Secondly, when the traveller 'smote' on the door, nobody answered whiche suggests that the listeners don't excist. Also, he used the phrase 'No head from the leaf-fringed sill' which suggests that you can't see them.

The ability to answer a direct question by making several clear points and supporting these by referencing the text, as well as adding any further explanations, is developed through a unit of work. By KS2, most children should be able to respond in this way. **Video clip 17** captures a Year 5's response to the question: *how does Shaun Tan portray a character's story?*

Demonstrate understanding of the core text through identifying the key focus in another text and responding

Having explored a key literary concept, such as how an author uses the setting to develop atmosphere, children should now be encouraged to read a new text and apply this knowledge. It is important that the text is simple enough for them to decode and understand, as well as mirroring the main focus of the unit. Where a text offers a significant challenge, children should be encouraged to read strategically in order to access the meaning. In some cases, the text could be read to the children to allow them to gather initial responses.

Once they have read the text a number of times, children should be encouraged to respond discursively, drawing on the explicit teaching and modelling taught in the **Investigation Phase**.

The following example shows a child from Warren Road Primary School in Orpington demonstrating their understanding of how an author uses the setting to create an atmosphere at the beginning of a novel. Having explored the opening pages of Kiran Millwood Hargrave's novel *The Island at the End of Everything*, the child was asked to respond to the opening of *Malamander* by Thomas Taylor. Their work has been typeset on the next page.

Malamander by Thomas Taylor

You've probably been to Eerie-on-Sea without ever knowing it. When you came it would have been summer. There would have been ice-cream and deckchairs and a seagull that pinched your chips. You probably poked about on rockpools with your mum whilst your dad found that funny shell – remember? And I bet that when you got in the car to drive home you looked at the words Cheerie-on-Sea written in lightbulb letters over the pier and got ready to forget all about your day at the seaside. It's that kind of place... in the summer.

But you should try being here when the first winter storms blow in when the letters C and H blow off the pier as they always do in November. When sea mist drifts up the streets like vast ghostly tentacles and salt-water spray rattles the windows of the Grand Nautilus Hotel. Few people visit Eerie-on-Sea then. Even the locals keep off the beach when darkness falls and the wind howls around more rocks and the wreck of the battle ship Leviathan where even now some swear that they have seen the umptious Malamander creep.

Child's response:

The setting reflects the mood of the story by the name: Eerie-on-Sea which gives a peculiar, negative feel which makes the reader ask questions like: 'Why is it called Eerie-on-Sea?' or 'Is there a bad side to this place?' It starts with that you've been there and you've enjoyed it then the second paragraph summarises that Eerie-on-Sea is not a place you'd want to be in winter; the contrast between the first and second paragraph is large. The first paragraph sets the mood of lovely and a nice place to visit in the summer; the second paragraph – however – sets a negative feel to the place and the only positive is the term 'Cheerie-on-Sea', but in winter, the positive disappears (the 'C' and 'H' fall off) and creates Eerie-on-Sea; the other names in that area also have an eerie and scary connotation.

Through this piece of discursive writing, the child is illustrating their ability to clarify the meaning of what they have read by:

- understanding the words in context;
- imagining and visualising the scene;
- tying information together;
- summarising key themes;
- thinking about what isn't explicitly stated.

This demonstrates their understanding of the way an author uses the setting to develop the atmosphere of the novel.

Demonstrate understanding through applying what they have learned in their own writing

To be able to write something in the style of a writer, a child needs to have noticed and internalised the techniques used to achieve the desired style and effect. It is the ability to understand how an author uses a variety of techniques that contribute to the overall purpose of a text.

Children in the EYFS may write a few sentences or have you scribe their ideas, drawing on a well-loved and closely read text. For some, the level and sophistication of the text will be too far above their writing capability. As children grow as writers, writing something similar and/or drawing on the author's style is an effective way to demonstrate understanding. It can show a child has grasped the author's use of pattern, word choice and sentence variation, alongside composition and effect.

Tyler, a Year 6 child from Chorley St James C. E. Primary School wrote this response to the opening prologue from *Malamander* shown earlier in this chapter (see **page 80**). He's used the same opening phrases, *"You've probably"* and introduced a contrast using *"But"*:

You've probably been on an airship when you went to the beach and felt the breeze against your face. Remember when you went on holiday and you got frightened when going up in the plane. I bet you have enjoyed going in a giant swimming pool with your friends and family. But you should also try going on a boat to go on holiday. When the sun beats down on your already hot and sweaty body. And some say there are sea giant creatures hidden down, swimming in the water. You probably won't believe this but some say they see giant boats in the air, in the distance.

Andrew, Year 6, from Thrussington Primary School responds to *Podkin One-Ear* by Kieran Larwood, setting his own extended story in a similar world. Here is an extract from his second chapter:

As the sun arose from the horizons and the birds sang their morning melodies, Pipkin woke from a rough night. The stone floor was not a comfortable mattress. Pasco and Prue were still slumbering deeply, so Pipkin decided to go and forage for food. He thought he should take the Moonclaw that he had found the previous night and, because it was more powerful, the fire core. Cautiously, he placed the amber gemstone into the heart of the handle and, like last night, the blade set alight. He ambled out of the gloomy cavern and stared around. A deep thick mist had settled on the ground making it incredibly hard to see. Because he had been unconscious the previous afternoon, he did not see his surroundings. It was a plain. The worst place to be. Pilgrimers could easily see them. Hopefully, the scouts would still be asleep. He patrolled the grasslands looking for any signs of food. After what felt like hours of foraging, he saw them. Orange carrots protruding from the fertile soil. He lunged forwards and ripped them out the ground and sprinted off, back to the cave.

He walked into the cave to see a very scared Pasco. "Thank the gods you came back. I thought you'd been killed or taken away. You could have at least left a note in the soil," she screamed.

"Sorry. I found some carrots and last night, when you were snoozing, I found the..." Pipkin started.

"MOONCLAW!" Pasco bellowed, "I thought that was mythical. At least we have some protection now." That was a seriously good point. Now, they could defend themselves against the scouts. Pipkin chucked four rather dirty carrots to Pasco thus to share with Prue. She brushed the soil off the carrot and started to eat. They munched on the fresh carrots that, thankfully, filled their stomachs. "Where do we go next?" Pasco asked.

"North to Mount Cloudreacher but I think we should go west to the forest first to make sure the prowling eyes of the Pilgrimers don't spot us," replied Pipkin. So it was that the three bunnies hopped off into the heart of the forest.

In the next example from Warren Road Primary School in Orpington, Connie (aged 11) demonstrates her understanding of the way Michelle Paver uses language to develop the voice of her characters in *Wolf Brother.* Through a close reading of the text, she was able to tune into the contrast in the characters' voices, manipulating her language choice to depict each character. This included the deep metaphorical imagery that is central to the voice of Wolf, shown in bold text below.

For a whole moon, we've been feasting on salmon. The herds of boar have migrated further South, leaving the Open Forest with hardly any prey. Fin-kedinn chose me to hunt for the clan, but even with my tracking skills, I've failed. Renn has tried to help, but the crunch of thick snow underfoot tells the Woodgrouse they're being hunted. So, they fly away. I remember the anger in Aki's voice: "Well done, Torak. I guess we'll have to starve thanks to your failure." I wish the boar would return.

Through the dense vegetation, the wind carries the scent of Forest-pig. In the Up, the wrath of the Sky-bear eats up the warm, bright Eye. My howl echoes in the darkness, bouncing off the trees, telling the forest that I'm hunting. The Thunderer throws his spears of light at the forest; as they feed on my surroundings, they turn into fire. Perfect. The crackle of flames and the applaud of the Thunderer will mask my scent as I tense my muscles, ready to pounce on the unsuspecting Forest-pig that has trotted into my cunning trap. My cubs shall feed like the Sky-bear tonight because a Wolf shows no mercy...

This piece from Epsom Primary School demonstrates how a child is bringing together his understanding of William Blake's *The Tyger* and David Almond's *Skellig*. In this instance, the child shows a rich understanding of the themes around creation posed by Blake, paired with the role of character that Almond has used to build intrigue. The transcript is included below.

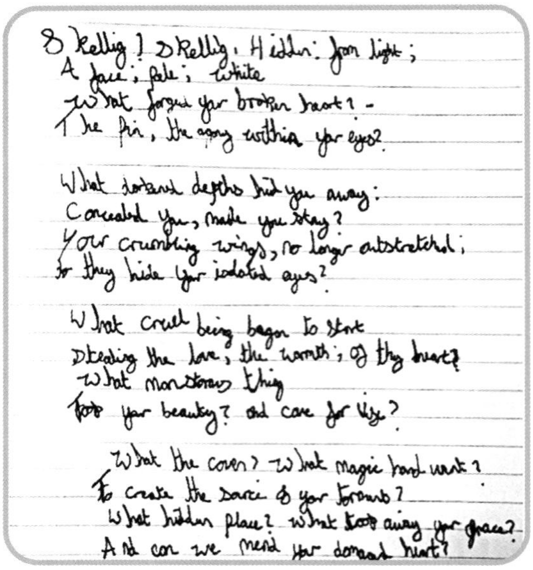

Skellig! Skellig. Hidden from light;
A face; pale; white
What forged your broken heart?
The pain, the agony within your eyes?

What darkened depths hid you away:
Concealed you, made you stay?
Your crumbling wings, no longer outstretched;
do they hide your isolated eyes?

What cruel being began to start
stealing the love, the warmth, of thy heart?
What monstrous thing
Took your beauty? And care for life?

What the coven? What magic hand want?
To create the source of your torment?
What hidden place? What took away your grace?
And can we mend your damaged heart?

Writing poetry in the same vein can be a very pleasing response, especially where the pattern does not constrain the imagination, as in this Year 6 example from Forest View Primary School, after work on Shakespeare's *Macbeth*.

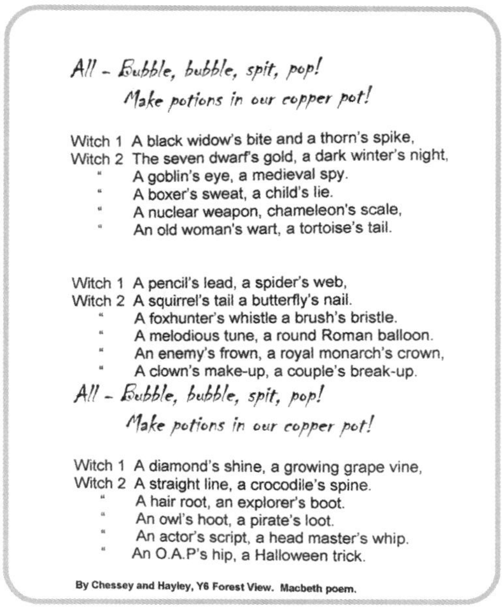

All – Bubble, bubble, spit, pop!
Make potions in our copper pot!

Witch 1 A black widow's bite and a thorn's spike,
Witch 2 The seven dwarf's gold, a dark winter's night,
" A goblin's eye, a medieval spy.
" A boxer's sweat, a child's lie.
" A nuclear weapon, chameleon's scale,
" An old woman's wart, a tortoise's tail.

Witch 1 A pencil's lead, a spider's web,
Witch 2 A squirrel's tail a butterfly's nail.
" A foxhunter's whistle a brush's bristle.
" A melodious tune, a round Roman balloon.
" An enemy's frown, a royal monarch's crown,
" A clown's make-up, a couple's break-up.

All – Bubble, bubble, spit, pop!
Make potions in our copper pot!

Witch 1 A diamond's shine, a growing grape vine,
Witch 2 A straight line, a crocodile's spine.
" A hair root, an explorer's boot.
" An owl's hoot, a pirate's loot.
" An actor's script, a head master's whip.
" An O.A.P's hip, a Halloween trick.

By Chessey and Hayley, Y6 Forest View. Macbeth poem.

The last example below is by Hattie in Year 6. The unit was focused on Chapter XII, *Inside Information* from Tolkien's *The Hobbit*. In the chapter, Bilbo comes face-to-face with the dragon Smaug, pretending to sleep with one eye open. The final challenge for the class was to rewrite the conversation from Smaug's point of view. The transcript follows on the next page.

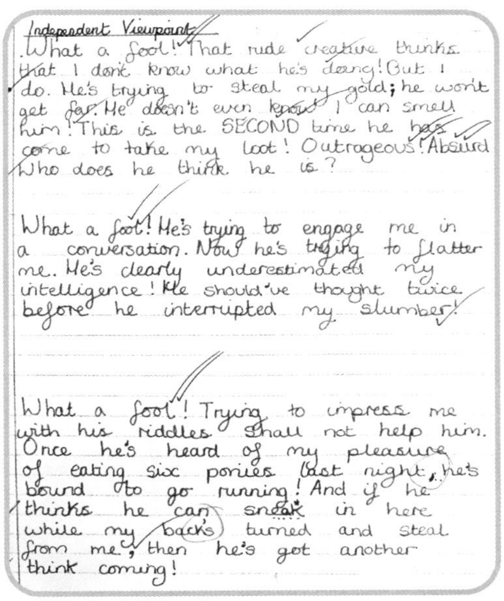

Independent Viewpoint
What a fool! That rude creative thinks that I don't know what he's doing! But I do. He's trying to steal my gold; he won't get far. He doesn't even know I can smell him! This is the SECOND time he has come to take my loot! Outrageous! Absurd! Who does he think he is?

What a fool! He's trying to engage me in a conversation. Now he's trying to flatter me. He's clearly underestimated my intelligence! He should've thought twice before he interrupted my slumber!

What a fool! Trying to impress me with his riddles. Shall not help him. Once he's heard of my pleasure of eating six ponies last night, he's bound to go running! And if he thinks he can sneak in here while my back's turned and steal from me, then he's got another think coming!

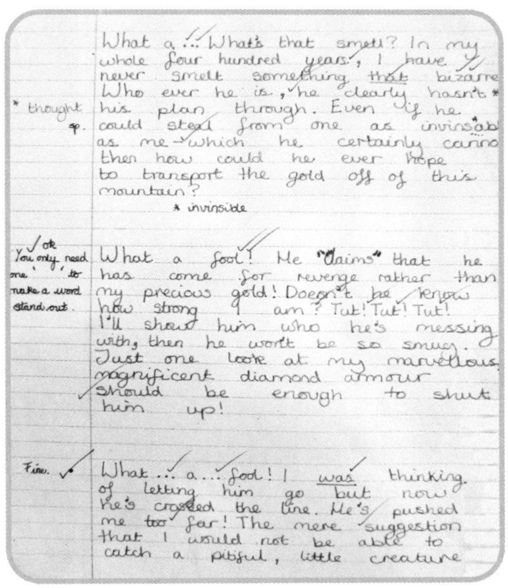

What a... What's that smell? In my whole four hundred years, I have never smelt something that bizarre. Who ever he is, he clearly hasn't thought his plan through. Even if he could steal from one as invinsable as me, which he certainly cannot, then how could he ever hope to transport the gold off of this mountain?

* thought sp.
* invincible

What a fool! He "claims" that he has come for revenge rather than my precious gold! Doesn't he know how strong I am? Tut! Tut! Tut! I'll show him who he's messing with, then he won't be so smug. Just one look at my marvellous magnificent diamond armour should be enough to shut him up!

ok You only need one ' to make a word stand out.

What... a... fool! I was thinking of letting him go but now he's crossed the line. He's pushed me too far! The mere suggestion that I would not be able to catch a pitiful, little creature

Fine.

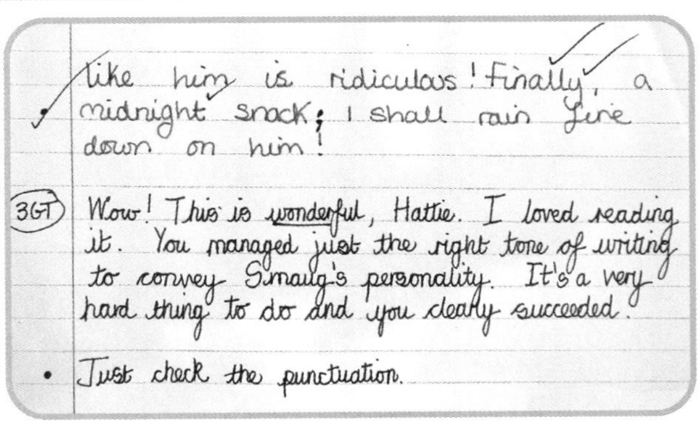

like him is ridiculous! Finally, a midnight snack; I shall rain fire down on him!

3GT Wow! This is wonderful, Hattie. I loved reading it. You managed just the right tone of writing to convey Smaug's personality. It's a very hard thing to do and you clearly succeeded.

• Just check the punctuation.

What a fool! That rude creature thinks that I don't know what he's doing! But I do. He's trying to steal my gold; he won't get far. He doesn't even know I can smell him! This is the SECOND time he has come to take my loot! Outrageous! Absurd! Who does he think he is?

What a fool! He's trying to engage me in a conversation. Now he's trying to flatter me. He's clearly underestimated my intelligence! He should've thought twice before he interrupted my slumber!

What a fool! Trying to impress me with his riddles shall not help him. Once he's heard of my pleasure of eating six ponies last night, he's bound to go running! And if he thinks he can sneak in here while my back's turned and steal from me, then he's got another think coming!

What a... What's that smell? In my whole four hundred years, I have never smelt something that bizarre! Who ever he is, he clearly hasn't thought his plan through. Even if he could steal from one as invincible as me – which he certainly cannot – then how could he ever hope to transport the gold off of this mountain?

What a fool! He 'claims' that he has come for revenge rather than my precious gold! Doesn't he know how strong I am? Tut! Tut! Tut! I'll show him who he's messing with, then he won't be so smug. Just one look at my marvellous, magnificent diamond armour should be enough to shut him up!

What... a... fool! I was thinking of letting him go but now he's crossed the line. He's pushed me too far! The mere suggestion that I would not be able to catch a pitiful, little creature like him is ridiculous! Finally, a midnight snack; I shall rain fire down on him!

Final points

By the end of a Talk for Reading unit, the children will have engaged deeply with a rich, worthwhile and deeply satisfying piece of great writing. They will have read carefully and learned how to tackle the demands of it, alongside learning that tenacity with a difficult text can be rewarding. It will have reinforced their understanding of different key literary concepts which will enrich their appreciation of other texts. They will have taken part in open discussions and shared and shaped their thinking with others, through learning to listen and being open to changing their ideas. After reading intensely and critically, they will have responded to the core text in various different ways demonstrating independent understanding.

Chapter 6: Things to consider when reading poetry

Pie Corbett

Fear of poetry

I've spent many years wondering why it is that so many of us are fearful of poetry. Perhaps it is simply because we are unfamiliar with it and not too sure how to approach it. We know how stories are told and what to expect from newspaper reports, letters, articles and information. However, most of our experience of poetry is limited to the school exam system and it is probably there that the problem lies.

Years ago, we learned that this strange poetry language was hard to understand, and we were taught to approach it as if it was a linguistic puzzle to be decoded. As the poet Billy Collins suggested, we were taught to strap the poem to a chair and try to thrash a meaning out of it. Most poetry teaching came down to spotting metaphors, underlining powerful verbs, identifying rhyming patterns and analysing the meaning. Furthermore, poems had one answer for the examiner. But of course, this is often blatantly untrue, because we can only respond in our own ways, based on what matters to us and making our own connections. Whilst words do not mean any old thing, for every individual there will be a myriad of possible links and associations echoing from their lives. The idea of just enjoying poetry in the same way that we might enjoy the class story, has probably become a faint memory that may have last been experienced in a Reception class when singing nursery rhymes.

I wonder what would happen if children were steeped in poetry so that from the Nursery onwards, it was an everyday occurrence, something to be enjoyed like music or singing? Would we collectively, children and teachers, lose that fear and know better how to experience poems, possibly not understanding everything, but happy to enjoy the music and the mystery? Perhaps then we could become more confident in our uncertainty. After all, I love Bob Dylan, but have no clue what he meant by a 'mercury mouth'.

As a child, my parents read me nursery rhymes from a very old collection. One of my favourites was a rhyme about *Babylon*:

How many miles to Babylon?
Three-score miles and ten.
Can I get there by candlelight?
Yes – and back again.

Beside the rhyme was a picture of a child dressed in nightclothes carrying a candle. I loved the sound of that poem. *Who is asking how many miles to Babylon and why?* Babylon sounded like a strange, mystical place. The answer seemed that it was far away, but it would be possible to get there. *How on earth could you travel in the dark, with just a candle, and get there and back again? Wouldn't the wind just blow the candle out?* In my head, Babylon was a magical city that could be travelled to at night; you just needed candlelight to take you there. I associated candles with magic and Christmas.

None of this I understood at the time, these were unvoiced thoughts jostling around. I just loved snuggling up with my Dad and the book and hearing his voice incant the rhyme. It was a magical, pleasurable nugget in my life. It is only on reflection that I can now tease away at what it meant for me. Nothing was ever explained, nothing needed to be explained, and yet it has stayed with me for 65 years. I was totally confident and happy in the poetry experience. My proposition is that because children do not experience poetry for pleasure, this becomes a barrier. Many remain unfamiliar with its language, unaware how to respond to its sound and meaning, let alone know that it can be a joy.

Years of poor teaching has reduced our experience to something fearful like an impenetrable verbal puzzle, an unfamiliar code to be cracked. Reading like a detective is not the way to read poetry. We need to begin by savouring rhymes and poems, by responding without fear not by some strange form of linguistic investigation. Daily rhymes and poems from the very start should build familiarity and help children become comfortable with the language and possibilities of poetry. This would begin with nursery rhymes, action rhymes and gradually move into the territory of poetry, in all its many guises. Poetry for pleasure is the key. If children's only experience of poetry is in the occasional 'unit' where a poem is disembowelled and dissected, no wonder most children do not like poetry or know how to respond.

"I think the more poems you read, the easier poetry is to understand."
Sophie, Year 6

On the other side of this rather bleak picture, there has been a great movement in the country, over the last 30 years or so, of poets working in schools. This movement has brought poetry alive for many children and intriguingly it seems that children love poetry under the right conditions. Poems can be enjoyed for themselves; for their music and meaning. Many of these poets have produced collections and edited anthologies of poetry that lie close to the experience of children, often in language that is instantly understandable. A poem like *Chocolate Cake* by Michael Rosen, provides no great barrier to understanding, but is a mesmeric joy that touches on the truth of a child's experience. Such poems act as stepping-stones into the wider world of poetry that, over time, create a love of poetry and lead steadily into more challenging territory.

How then do we deepen the poetic experience? Firstly, we have to accept that more demanding poems, such as *The Listeners* by Walter de la Mare, can be appreciated before understanding – in the same way that I loved *Babylon* but didn't really grasp the meaning of it. The skilful teacher paves the way into comprehension and appreciation by planning activities that will help children find ways into a poem. This might be through performance, drama, discussion, art, dance, music or focused tasks that help children grow closer to the poem, whilst steadily deepening understanding.

The poetry reader often has to be confident in their uncertainty, not concerned by the pressure for immediate understanding. That is not how poetry always works. Poems are experiences. For instance, I have loved T.S. Eliot's *The Love Song of Alfred J Prufrock* for half a century, but much of it remains a wonderful and strange mystery to me. Poems do not always present themselves as a clear narrative or simple statement that proceeds in a logical manner. Poems often hint and suggest, creating echoes in the memory. If we can learn to enjoy the words, the sound, the images, atmospheres, and suggestions that poems provoke over the years, then perhaps children and teachers would be more ready to engage with tougher material.

Building a poetry curriculum

Reading and performing helps us internalise language and possibilities – it increases our range of voices to call upon when writing. As teachers, we need to put into the minds of children the voices of many poets and poems for them to draw on when creating, so they have internalised a massive bank of poetic possibility. Each poem becomes a block of knowledge, a frame of reference.

> ***"Reading poetry makes my imagination run wild. Our 'poem of the week' has introduced me to so many new poems, ideas and images, and has helped enrich my vocabulary."***
> Gweni, Year 6, Coastlands Community Primary School

Work out which poets and poems are going to become the main focus for teaching over the primary years. This means that the children become familiar with a range of poets over time. As a school, agree on and resource a poetry spine with key poets and poems for each term. Establish a 'rhyme/poem of the week' across the school to ensure that children hear and perform lots of poetry. Make sure that poetry books are readily available.

"Having a big pile of books to flick through, I'll always find one I like; I look for poetry books that others might not know about; I love 'Poem of the Day' because you can do it with your friends, you can find and practise poems together; it's important to practise so you get the words right; our best afternoons are when we get all the poetry books out and sit and read them with each other."

Jon Biddle's class

Jon Biddle's collection for Year 5

"When we read our 'poem of the week' together I really enjoy sharing it with my friends. I would say to children who haven't read much poetry before to not be scared – to be brave, because a poem can mean different things to different people so your ideas can't be wrong. Reading and writing poems helps you block out the rest of the world."

Georgie, Year 4, Coastlands Community Primary School

Choosing poetry for teaching

Much of the poetry published over the last 20 years is easy to understand and whilst the poems might be fun to read, their impact may be brief. Poems for use in lessons have to earn their place in the curriculum. Poetry teaching deepens the relationship between the reader and the poem. Great poems, poems that have survived the years, may help us come closer to eternal truths about ourselves and our world, exploring the human condition as well as bringing fresh ways to experience ourselves and the world. Choose quality poetry that challenges and stands the test of time, e.g. *The Listeners* by Walter de la Mare, *The Tyger* by William Blake, *Jabberwocky* by Lewis Carroll, *What are Heavy?* by Christina Rossetti.

In order to develop critical and strategic readers of poetry, take the poem you have selected for your class and follow the teaching sequence described in **Chapters 3-5**. Examples of poetry unit overviews can be found in **Chapter 8**. Below are some further elements to consider when working with a poem.

The importance of reading aloud and performance

To understand a poem, we have to actively engage, recreating the poem inside our minds, making it our own by relating it to our real and imagined experience. Poems have to be read aloud to experience the musicality and meaning. The written poem is like a musical score that comes alive when the poem is spoken aloud, so that has to be our starting point.

> ***"When we start a new poem of the week, it's sometimes difficult but it gets easier the more we say it. Often, I know them off by heart by the end of the week."***
> Jason, Year 6, Coastlands Community Primary School

The first encounter with a poem will be through you reading it to the class. As children become familiar with the poem, it is important that they are given time to prepare and recite it for themselves, either individually or in groups. During this time, they will naturally begin to try and interpret the poem, thinking about how it should be spoken. The key is to 'vary' the pace, rhythm, expression and volume in relation to meaning. Perform the poem in any of the following ways:

- create class audio or film clips;
- read it to other classes or in assembly;
- use percussive instruments to accompany the words as they are said aloud to feel the rhythm.

We may never fully understand Blake's *The Tyger*, but we can learn it by heart and love the mystery. Do not be afraid to make the poem live. The more poetry lives fearlessly, the more the children will love poetry without fear.

Deepening understanding through oral comprehension

Discussion is essential as it is through talk that we may begin to bring into being what we think about a poem. It helps if you model **thinking aloud** about a poem. At this point you would consider and reveal what has drawn you to a poem, which bits you enjoy, which aspects 'speak' to your experience. Share too, the mysteries or parts that are hard – these can be put to one side, remaining uncertain at the moment. Explain what interests or surprises you; talk about the word choices and imagery; the pictures a poem paints; the memories or ideas that it triggers; as well as the patterns that add to the pleasure and meaning.

> ***"If someone finds reading poems hard, I would tell them to read it again and talk about it with your friends because this will make it easier."***
>
> Jason, Year 5, Chorley St James' C of E Primary School

Exploratory and tentative dialogic talk helps a class grow understanding and deepen appreciation. You can trigger the discussion with an open question such as, *"What can we say about this?"* Show a genuine interest in the poem and what the children say. Orchestrate the discussion so the class have a chance to deepen their understanding. Coax out initial ideas, including what the class enjoyed or what the poem made them think about. Encourage them to share the feelings or memories it evoked. All ideas should be accepted and given consideration. If the comments move away from the poem behind or become 'wild', return to the poem.

> **What do you do when you struggle with a poem?**
>
> ***"Sometimes I leave it for a while and then go back to it; I think it's OK not to understand a poem straight away, I might get a little clue the first time I read it and then think about it; sometimes poems aren't meant to be understood anyway; it's really important to talk, to your friends and see what they think; you have to understand what the words mean as part of the whole poem, don't just look at one word at a time; I always write on poems and mark places I'm not sure about."***
>
> Jon Biddle's class

Through sharing ideas, the class will gradually deepen their understanding of what the poem might offer. Slow the pace of discussion and use bit-by-bit reading to help the children tie clues together and gradually build up the movement through the poem.

> ***"If you haven't read much poetry before, it can be difficult to understand, but re-read the poem, think it through and the meaning becomes clearer."***
> Gweni, Year 6, Coastlands Community Primary School

Comprehension grids are useful for getting the discussion going. Use headings such as:

- Feelings
- Thoughts
- Best word, line or image
- A line I'd like to have written
- Mysteries
- Riddles
- Confusions
- Surprises
- Links to life
- Links to other texts
- Memories
- Pictures in my head
- Images – similes/metaphors
- Symbols
- Themes
- Poetry patterns

Responding to poetry

It is important to help children dig under the skin of a poem, with some form of interaction. In addition to the response activities listed in **Chapter 4**, here are a few other activities that you might like to consider. Remember to match the activity to the poem, considering what might help children think more intensely and at what point the activity will have the greatest impact.

- **Titling** – remove the title from the poem and present the poem to the class. The children can then read it and decide, in pairs or threes, what it might be called and provide evidence for their thinking.
- **Cut up** – cut up a poem by words, lines or verses and put it into a different order. The children can reorganise the fragments into a coherent whole. In Tennyson's poem on the next page, I have cut the lines in half and jumbled them up to be pieced back together.

The Eagle
he falls.
with crooked hands;
close to the sun
beneath him crawls;
in lonely lands,
ring'd with the azure world,
from his mountain walls,
the wrinkled sea
he stands.
he clasps the crag
he watches
and like a thunderbolt

Alfred Tennyson

You could try this with a poem you are studying in class.

- **Cloze procedure** – omit key words from a poem to create a cloze activity. The children fill in the blanks thinking about the rhythm, meaning and style. Try these famous lines from Shakespeare's *Macbeth*.
  Fire burn and cauldron bubble.
  Fillet of a ______ Snake,
  In the cauldron boil and bake;
  ______ of newt and ______ of frog,
  ______ of bat and ______ of dog,
  Adder's ______ and blindworm's ______,
  Lizard's ______ and owlet's ______.
- **Rewrite** – present a poem as prose and ask the children to re-structure it into the lines of a poem, considering where each line or verse break might fall. Here is an example:
  Owl was darker than ebony, flew through the night eyes like amber searchlights, rested on a post, feathers wind-ruffled, stood stump-still, talons ready to seize and squeeze. Owl was death that swamped the fields for it flew through the dark that tightened its knot that bandaged the hills in a blindfold of fear. Owl flew – who – who – who –
- **Underline** – children could read, discuss and underline or highlight memorable, interesting or bewildering but beautiful aspects of the poem for further discussion. Take my mesostic riddle poem on the next page.

Animal Riddle

*Like a small **B**ear it*
*bundles over the d**A**rk road,*
brushes past the front gate,
as if she owns the joint.
*rolls the **D**ustbin*
like an expert barrel rider.
*Tucks into yesterday's **G**arbage,*
crunches worms for titbits.
*Wakes us from deep sl**E**ep,*
blinks back at torchlight.
*Our midnight feaste**R**,*
ghost-friend,
moon-lit,
zebra bear.

- **Respond in another form** – here is part of an invented dictionary definition by Year 5, in response to *Jabberwocky* by Lewis Carroll:
  A vorpal sword is the most deadly weapon ever made by man. The handle has encrusted diamonds included in its pure gold. Although it may look very small, a press of the green diamond will let it become extendable to at least 6ft! A special feature is hidden beneath the sword; it is a poison stick. One press of the red diamond and it shoots out at the speed of light. Deadliness 85/100.
- **Respond through the arts** – set poems to music or percussion. Poems could also be acted, illustrated, painted or even turned into a model.

All these activities encourage children to talk about and engage more deeply with poetry. How we approach a poem depends on thinking about what will be the best way into it.

Our aim is to develop an inclination towards poetry with its surprises, emotion, mystery, music and beauty. Try to avoid summoning the implements of grammatical and exam torture and applying them to poetry! Poetry should bring serious joy.

Chapter 7: Things to consider when reading non-fiction

Pie Corbett

Story, theatre and poems fill the human spirit and often help us witness things both within and outside of our own experiences. They deepen our understanding of ourselves and others and bind us together as a world culture. Everyone loves a good story and around the world, common patterns and concerns arise because, in the end, we are all just people.

Non-fiction also feeds the spirit, but in a different way. This is the realm of adding to our store of knowledge about things that matter or interest us. This might be finding out how to do things, explaining why things happen, as well as the opportunity to consider ideas, follow lines of argument and be persuaded to different viewpoints or actions. Through non-fiction, we find out more about our world. It is what helps us all 'get by', from following directions, to catching the right train, to deepening our understanding of conflicts around the world.

In **Chapter 4**, we discussed the idea that children need to be strategic readers so that they notice when understanding is falling apart and know how to slow down, re-read, seek out the main ideas and summarise bit-by-bit to help understanding. In non-fiction, the notion of teaching children to read strategically really gains traction. Non-fiction texts are not read in the same way as fiction. To read effectively, you have to know how to choose the right text and then find your way round that text for whatever purpose you may have as a reader.

It is worth remembering that non-fiction is very much driven by audience and purpose. These aspects determine the content, structure and style of the writing. As readers, we should think about: *who wrote it? What did they need to know and why did they write it? Who might read it and why?* This sets up our expectations as readers.

In Talk for Reading schools, the units studied balance fiction, poetry and non-fiction over the year. However, one other core approach has been to ensure that daily, across the school, children read when studying other subjects, from PE to art. This can be done very simply, by ensuring that in sessions throughout the curriculum there are always a few sentences that relate to what is being learned. This not only reinforces subject learning, but also means that over seven years there is daily teaching of non-fiction reading, that threads in all the key aspects that need to be learned. This should be brief and not take over subject teaching and learning.

It is useful to map out where children will be taught different aspects of non-fiction reading in the curriculum overview, so that their ability to locate and make sense of information becomes increasingly sophisticated. The table below sets out the core aspects to be learned and may help to provide sharper focus for what needs to be taught. It is not hierarchical and therefore not organised in terms of importance.

Core skill	What to do

How to find the right place to read	• Select from the title/blurb – is this book going to be interesting or provide the information or ideas that I am looking for?
	• Use the macro text structure to locate specifics:
	  • contents;
	  • index;
	  • chapter headings;
	  • sub-headings.

How to read closely, efficiently and effectively	• Skim to get the general idea. • Scan to locate specific information. • Tie together pieces of information located in different places. • Use conjunctions, adverbials and generalisers to aid reading, e.g. *Most people think...*; *However, ...*; *A key argument is that...*; *On the other hand...* • Find the main ideas, points or arguments. • Understand the details that back up the main ideas. • Learn how to paraphrase ideas and take notes effectively.
How to read graphics	• Interpret diagrams, images, graphs and photos.
How to read critically	• Consider the difference between facts and opinions. • Consider what is relevant/irrelevant. • Consider author bias. • Consider where a text offers contrasts, counter arguments, alternative ideas. • Consider whether the author is a reliable source. • Compare with other texts on a similar topic. • Think analytically about what the text says.
After reading	• Know which sections to revisit for more close re-reading and where understanding might be tenuous. • Learn how to double-check facts by looking at other texts. • Generate other related areas for investigation.
Summarising and evaluating	• Make connections with what you already know and other texts say. • Summarise what has been learned in your own words, with your own viewpoint. • Evaluate the text and its contents.

This all needs to be modelled by you and practised by the children, using interesting, challenging texts. A dialogic approach, where the class can have a deep discussion, is probably more relevant to texts that set out to discuss, persuade or explore ideas, views and lines of argument. Straightforward facts will not give much room for deep discussions, other than understanding clearly what has been said and its relevance. However, discursive texts, persuasive texts and those that explore thinking will be rich with opportunity. This is especially true at a high level when talking about philosophical ideas, for instance, or difficult moral problems.

Engaging with the text

Start with a **hook** which may well set up something we need to know more about or provide a rich context. You may have one core text or several texts about the same subject, allowing for comparison. This then leads into the routine of reading and re-reading to the class and taking **initial responses**. It is worth experimenting with different headings in comprehension grids, depending on the text:

New information	Things I know already	My opinions
What surprised me?	Any bias?	What made me wonder?
Questions I'm left with	How did it make me feel?	Who is the audience?
What is the purpose?	Who might be interested?	What did the author need to know?
Key points I remember	Key sentence starters and patterns	How is it organised?
Ideas for how to best read this	What interested me?	What I've learned
Anything I agree with/ disagree with?	What is useful?	How might this be used?
Summary	Connections with my life	Links to other texts
Related memories	Related experiences	Facts or opinions
Things I want to tell others	Things I want to discuss	Best/worst part of the text

Never-heard-the-word

The History of Crime and Punishment – Year 5

Keywords	Never heard	Heard – not sure of meaning	Know what it means (jot down meaning)
primary source	✓		
secondary source	✓		
flogging			whipping
bias	✓		
corporal punishment		✓	
gallows		✓	
pillory		✓	
defendant			defender
execution			to kill someone
sentence		✓	
victim		✓	
hearsay			rumour
verdict			judgement

Initial work will almost certainly lead you into looking at technical vocabulary and may well involve further context setting. If there is any key technical language that you would like them to acquire then using a 'never-hear-the-word grid' would be important, as shown in this image.

The unit may link to a class trip or a visiting speaker on the topic or the wider curriculum. It may also provide background knowledge to an English unit of work. For instance, a story like *Jack and the Beanstalk* should be planned to be read in the spring when beans could be grown, science work on growth carried out, and the reading and writing of instructions taught. It is worth remembering that the focus should be on teaching reading comprehension, as opposed to prioritising learning the topic (though this may well be a bonus aspect). Learning how to read non-fiction strategically will enable children to apply what they learn to their own independent reading.

Deepening understanding through oral comprehension

Gradually, the children's understanding of the text will begin to deepen. In the main, you will be mining the text to extract the information it holds, the issues that it presents, or the way it attempts to persuade the reader. Almost certainly, you will be exploring the tone of the writing which should relate to the intended audience. It may be formal or informal and written in a certain way for a specific audience. A comparison between the recipes of Jamie Oliver and Delia Smith soon shows a more informal, 'matey' tone from Oliver as he is targeting younger cooks! Jamie *chivvies eggs round the pan* whereas Delia *stirs gently*!

Teaching children how to use the structure of a non-fiction text to locate information is a key aspect to non-fiction work. This will be both at a whole text, macro level (e.g. using the index) or at micro level (e.g. how to use sentence signposts such as, *"The main idea..."* to aid reading efficiently). In many texts, key facts or ideas are found at different points, so children need to be taught to locate information across a text and tie it together. An important part of comprehending non-fiction texts hinges around being able to identify the main ideas, themes or arguments and understand what lies behind them. Much work has to be done on distinguishing between minor or supportive points being made and the big idea.

It is almost impossible to write non-fiction without bias. As children move through the primary school, they should become more experienced in considering the author's viewpoint and how bias might be used intentionally or unintentionally to promote ideas and manipulate the reader. This is vital because children are bombarded daily by the media and need to develop a critical stance – to understand that not everything you read or hear is actually to be taken for truth. This is why when working with non-fiction, studying several texts on the same topic is useful. A simple task is to take one current news story and compare how it is presented in a range of newspapers. I remember doing this with a Year 6 class, where one child made the comment, *"well, somebody's not telling the truth!"*

Response activities

Response activities may help children make connections to ideas and information, linking to their own experiences and what they know. We often play 'Professor Know-it-all' with children to get them to know the text well. This involves a volunteer from the class acting in character as an 'expert'. They extract key points and supportive information from the text to present it to the rest of the class, and then answer any questions the other children may have. There is skill in both having extracted and understood the main point and supportive factors and being able to use technical language correctly. Another useful activity for information texts is to get the children to underline key features and use these to label an image or diagram. For instance, children might read the following description of what a Roman legionnaire wore and then use the facts to label a picture, as in the example on the next page.

Roman legionaries had to be ready to fight, but also able to move swiftly and often travel for long distances. They wore leather sandals with hob nails on the soles. In the summer, they wore red tunics made out of breathable linen to keep them cool. They wore the same style and colour tunics in winter, but the tunics were much thicker and warmer as they were made out of wool. On top of their tunics, they wore metal shoulder plates and body armour which was made of iron. These must have been very heavy. To protect their heads, they wore a helmet. They carried huge shields made of red and brown painted wood and leather which were curved to protect them in battle. They also carried a javelin as well as their sword.

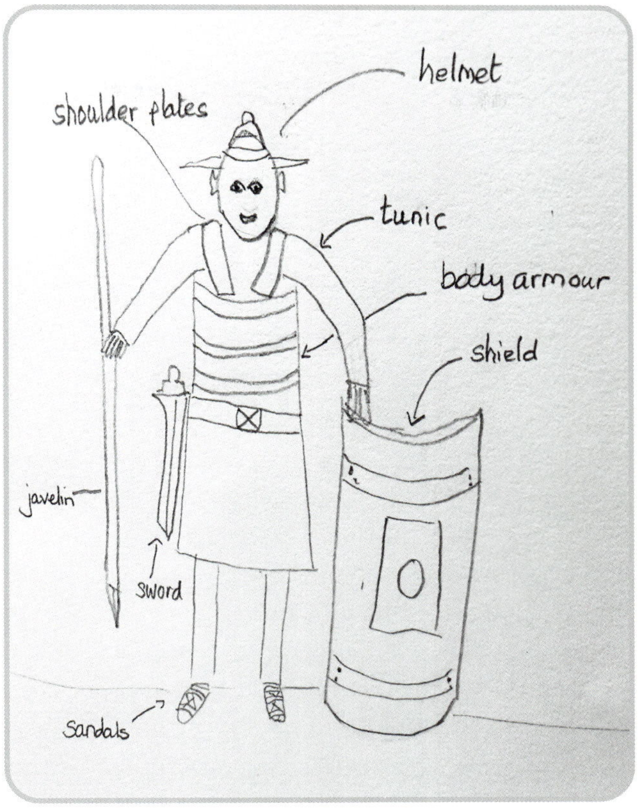

In **Handout 4 (online)**, there are other example of useful response activities when reading non-fiction.

Summarising and evaluating

Summarising across a text and building up to understanding the main ideas is also key in non-fiction.

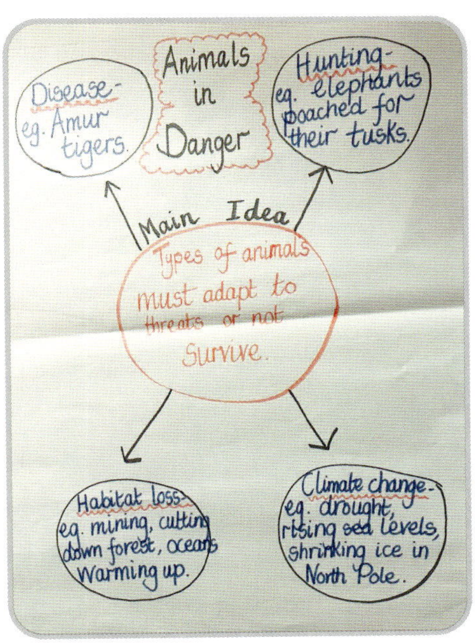

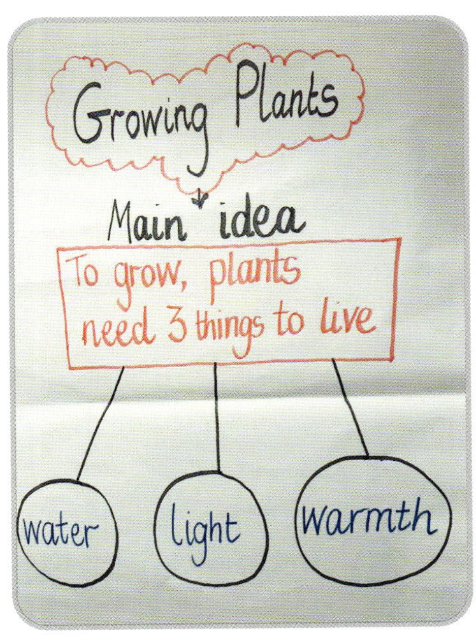

Evaluation matters because we need to know who to listen to! *What makes an author trustworthy? Who has the background experience?* Discussions should be held to develop children's critical stance, including looking at when it was published and considering whether the writer is sufficiently knowledgeable. Children should think about whether the text was worth spending time on, as well as what they learned from it. They might reflect upon how the text would be used and by whom.

Final points

Topic work was popular around 50 years ago and still prevails in many schools. I still see topic books in primary schools which look gorgeous: colour photocopying; templates coloured in; every book with the same graphs, images, details and... writing copied from the board or from books. This may look fancy, but it is a waste of time. Children have to process information in different ways in order to 'make it their own' and learn. In Talk for Reading, we place an emphasis on locating the relevant information and then getting the children to process this in different ways so that they can internalise it. This comes through teaching them how to highlight and underline important points, as well as showing them how to take notes, so that they become skilled at identifying the core ideas or facts with supporting detail. This key information could then be presented in different ways, including:

- producing a fact box;
- writing true or false statements;
- creating a glossary;
- drawing and labelling a diagram;
- providing counter arguments to the author's viewpoint;
- making a short film clip;
- preparing a PowerPoint presentation;
- explaining the information within the text to a partner;
- writing an article about the topic using information from the text.

It is through re-processing the text that children are ultimately able to understand it. Copying is a waste of time and does not aid comprehension.

One of the most common enquiries that I receive runs along the following lines:

> ***"I am doing a topic on rivers, do you know a good picture book/novel that I can read to the class?"***

Novels are fiction. They are made up. Their purpose is not to convey information about rivers or explain erosion, sedimentation and ox bow lakes. That can be found best by reading non-fiction, using internet resources and visiting a river. Indeed, relying on a fiction book to provide information about a topic may well actually teach children misconceptions and potentially promote worrying views if taken at face value. *The Boy in the Striped Pyjamas* by John Boyne is a good case in point. Those concerned with Holocaust studies at an academic level have serious concerns that the book portrays worrying myths if taken as a form of truth. However, despite arguing this many times, teachers persist in the strange idea that linking a story to a subject enhances learning. It usually means selecting a weaker reading text and adds almost nothing. Worse still, it may even perpetrate various myths about the subject. Given the variety of excellent non-fiction texts, there is no need for making such tenuous links.

Chapter 8: Unit overviews

Jamie Thomas

This chapter contains four units of work that exemplify the teaching sequence. They capture the thinking that needs to take place when preparing a Talk for Reading unit. Please note that planning does not always fit neatly into a grid; sometimes elements get left out or are minimal as the text does not require them. Avoid filling in boxes because they are there and focus on how to teach the text to get the most out of it and move children towards understanding it at a deeper level. You may find, for instance, that aspects of the **Investigation Phase** start on day one because someone is bursting to talk deeply about an aspect of the text. This is fine as teaching is often instinctive and involves picking up on what is happening, and this cannot always be planned for.

Talk for Reading texts

1. *Voices in the Park* by Anthony Brown
    - Background context notes
    - The initial brainstorm around literacy concepts
    - Phase 1 Introduction to the text
    - Phase 2 Investigation of the text
    - Phase 3 Independent understanding
2. *Overheard on a Saltmarsh* by Harold Monro
    - Background context notes
    - The initial brainstorm around literacy concepts
    - Phase 1 Introduction to the text
    - Phase 2 Investigation of the text
    - Phase 3 Independent understanding
3. *Fox* by Margaret Wild and Ron Brooks
    - Background context notes
    - The initial brainstorm around literacy concepts
    - Phase 1 Introduction to the text
    - Phase 2 Investigation of the text
    - Phase 3 Independent understanding
4. *Invictus* by William Ernest Henley
    - Background context notes
    - The initial brainstorm around literacy concepts
    - Phase 1 Introduction to the text
    - Phase 2 Investigation of the text
    - Phase 3 Independent understanding

1. *Voices in the Park* by Anthony Browne

Background context notes

Anthony Browne was a previous Children's Laureate and one of the foremost makers of picture books. He has spent many hours watching gorillas in a wildlife park and, if you're familiar with his stories, you'll know they often feature apes playing the role of humans. He is also famous for his surreal and playful illustrations. The books are part of a game he plays with the readers. In his illustrations, he draws on famous works of art, but he also hides surprising images so that, for example, a tree takes on the shape of a hat – or footprints become leaves.

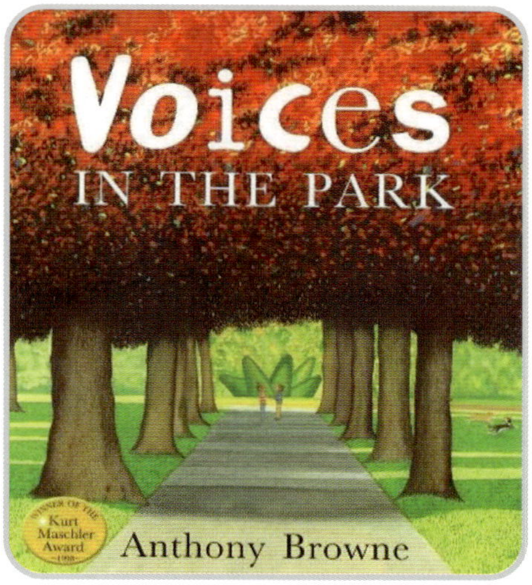

The initial brainstorm around literacy concepts

Role of characters/issues/information (as applicable)

The story explores a day in the life of four main characters who take a trip to the park. Each of the characters has a 'voice' and retells their versions of the events that take place. What becomes apparent, is the radically different perspectives that are presented, providing ample opportunity to explore issues such as stereotyping, prejudice and socioeconomic status. The story also explores the delicate topics of friendship and diversity.

Role of setting/mood/tone (as applicable)

Whilst the park is the central to the story, the images in the book position the reader to see the multiple perspectives of what actually happens. The author uses the seasons to mirror the characteristics of each voice: a wealthy, uptight woman in the autumn; an unhappy and unemployed man in the winter; a lonely boy in the spring; and a carefree young girl in the summer. In addition, each image has inferred meaning about the character, be it through the use of colour and tone to show emotion, or references to other works of art, such as Edvard Munch's painting *The Scream*. The illustrations are in fact as influential as the words, and need to be explored in depth.

Structure of text – how the text works

The story is written in four chapters, or through four voices, each with their own voice and font. Time should be spent looking at how this affects us as readers. It may be worth considering the order of the voices and whether this has any impact on our connection with the characters. Both the words and pictures have significant importance when reading the story and children should consider which images are pivotal in their understanding of the key events.

Use of language, including figurative language

Whilst the text is relatively simple, a lot can be inferred by the voices of the characters. Browne uses symbolism and metaphorical representation through the artwork, and children will need time to make these connections in the text.

Perspectives/viewpoints – author/narrator/character/reader

The entire book is rooted in the exploration of viewpoint, with four characters recalling the key events of their time in the park. It's important to try to empathise with each character, considering their own motives, perceptions and emotions. The story also offers the opportunity to look at how different readers may interpret the text, i.e. *how might girls, boys, fathers, mothers, unemployed people, etc. interpret the text?*

Main themes/ideas/arguments

Voices in the Park explores a number of important themes, such as stereotyping, prejudice, socioeconomic status, alienation, friendship, diversity and different viewpoints.

As you can see, the initial brainstorming opens up the vast potential of the book. Before exploring the story with the children, clarify what you want the children to have learned by the end of the unit. This will involve deciding which of the literary concepts will be the main focus. Having done this, craft your unit synopsis.

The unit synopsis

By the end of the unit, children may be able to:

- discuss how authors present different viewpoints of similar experiences;
- talk about how authors use illustrations to create an impact on the reader;
- empathise with characters and talk or write in role.

Phase 1 – Introduction to the text

> **The Introduction Phase**
>
> Achieve basic understanding:
>
> **Before reading**
> - hook;
> - context;
> - activate prior knowledge.
>
> **While reading**
> - teacher models reading with fluency;
> - prediction;
> - initial responses;
> - re-reading;
> - initial vocabulary;
> - literal retrieval;
> - establish focus.

To hook the children in, you may like to find and discuss the original images, films and books that are referenced in the text, such as *The Scream* by Edvard Munch, *The Laughing Cavalier* by Frans Hals, *Mary Poppins*, *King Kong* and *Narnia*.

Show the cover and read the title to the class. You may like to begin with a **prediction**: *what do the children think the book is going to be about?* Many children suggest that it is to do with friendship because there are two dogs who want to play together and two children who want to play together. Make a list of ideas. These can be revisited after reading the book.

On initial reading, gather the children in close so that they can see the illustrations or use multiple copies of the book. Show each page and read the book straight through without stopping. **Model reading with fluency**, thinking about using expression and intonation to portray the different characters.

Gather the children's **initial responses**, thoughts, ideas and any aspects that surprise them. Jot down any comments on the flipchart.

Re-read the story several times with children joining in as they become familiar with the book. Pause for further reactions, discussion, responses and ideas. Try saying different lines in different ways and talk about which seems most appropriate and why.

Get children to identify any **vocabulary** that needs further discussion, e.g. *pedigree, Labrador, mongrel, shooed, whatsoever, frightful types, rough-looking, energy, waste of time, boring, slide, silly twit, wimp, bandstand*. Explore the meaning of the vocabulary in context, providing simple definitions that can be orally rehearsed. Make sure that the children practise using the new words in context to cement understanding.

Go through each of the four sections of the book in turn, asking basic literal retrieval questions, e.g. *where did they go for a walk?* Expect other points of discussion to arise.

Phase 2 – Investigation of the text

Take each double-page spread in turn and spend time looking at every one carefully. This could be done in groups with each group presenting to the class what they have noticed. Use **oral comprehension** to explore and develop ideas. The need to slip into a dialogic approach will occur on many occasions with such a rich text.

The Investigation Phase

Deepen understanding of the focus through:

- oral comprehension;
- strategic reading;
- response activities;
- exploring structure and effect;
- summarising;
- evaluating;
- reading fluently.

Model how to use **strategic reading** to look at the images closely and gain the most from the text. Then work with the class together to get them carefully 'reading the image', before finally letting the children do this independently. This could lead into writing about the images. You could provide them with a range of sentence starters, such as:

- *In this image, Anthony Browne is...*
- *The image of... suggests that...*
- *The use of bright colours suggests that...*

You could also encourage the children to consider:

- how the characters are shown;
- what the colours and images suggest to the reader about the characters;
- how the images make the reader feel;
- the pictorial ideas that are playful and those that suggest something meaningful that aids understanding;
- the references to famous paintings, ideas from stories (*Narnia*) or films (*Mary Poppins, King Kong*);
- the image they think is most important and why.

It is also worth extending work on images to also include reading the design of the page. Encourage the children to think about:

- the use of colour, light and dark;
- the positioning of characters on the page;
- the different fonts in the four different sections used to create different moods;
- the use of space on the pages, especially where a strong vertical line is used to split up characters or to establish a connection (such as a lamppost or slide).

Raise questions to investigate with the class, such as: *how does Anthony Browne present different viewpoints of similar experiences and use illustrations to create an impact on the reader?* Devise **response activities** to explore the question and build understanding of viewpoint. Below are some ideas.

- Allocate an individual 'voice' to groups within the class and ask them to make a list of ideas about the different characters' viewpoints.
- Hot-seat each character in turn to help the children understand the different perspectives.
- Invite a child to be in role as a character and make a phone call to a friend.
- Discuss with the children what they think each character thinks about the other three.
- Draw a 'thought bubble' on the flipchart and fill it with ideas from the class to show what each character is thinking. Contrast characters' views about the same things.
- Draw the links between characters.
- Hold a class discussion on why the characters might behave as they do.
- Create a 'freeze frame' of an image from the story with children in role as the characters, and then interview them about what they are thinking and feeling.
- Hold an 'advice surgery' where volunteers from the class play each character and discuss their problems.
- Write a class diary entry together – or a letter in role as a character.
- Write a note from Charles to Smudge – or the other way round. Use the flipchart to capture ideas and then compose the letter together.

You could also use shared writing to model how to summarise the class's thinking and write discursively about selected characters, exploring what they are like and how they view the world and each other differently. Guide the children to give evidence from the text to support their views. For example:

The character that interested me most is the boy, Charles. It appears that he has no father, and his mother is very dominant, perhaps trying to fill the role of a father. She seems to be more concerned for her pet dog and, in the section from her viewpoint, the dog is mentioned before Charles. She says, 'It was time to take Victoria, our pedigree Labrador, and Charles, our son, for a walk.' Later on, she treats Charles more like the dog and uses 'please' when talking to the dog! She says, "Charles, come here. At once!" but to the dog she calls out, "And come here please, Victoria."

The initial image in Charles's section is in muted colours and the character tells the reader that he is bored. In both the first two images, Charles appears isolated which creates a strong sense of loneliness.

When considering structure and effect, you could introduce a fifth character into the mix. This might be done through children choosing from a set of images. They could then write a storyboard in the style of the book using the chosen images, aiming to let the reader know how the new character feels about the other characters, as well as how they view what is happening. The children should concentrate on:

- the new character's relationship to the four other characters in the book;
- what the new character will do in the park (play with the children, talk to the grown-ups, watch from a distance, etc.).

Here is an example from a Year 6 child at Penn Wood Primary School in Slough.

Onlooker perspective

As I walk around, I can see many people: families, ~~parents~~ dog walkers and many kids playing around. But for some odd reason I can't take my eyes off this impertinent woman. Seems as if she is looking over this man. In ~~an~~ a serious judgemental gaze. I notice that the man and woman are ignoring each other on purpose. The male is looking at a newspaper and looks to be searching for something important. I wonder why this man has chosen this particular seat on the bench. In the distance I hear ~~a~~ lots of children playing but I see two kids glancing at that pair that is near the bench.

An alternative way of exploring viewpoint through writing would be to take one of the characters and rewrite their section altering their viewpoint. For example:

I'd had a great morning mucking about with Victoria at home when Mummy said that it was time to go for a walk to my favourite place – the park.

As soon as we got there, Victoria rushed off to play with a friendly dog and I looked around to see if there were any other children that I could play with on the swings and slide. There was a girl called Smudge and we decided to play on the slide. She was a bit scared, but I showed her how to use it and soon we were both whizzing down, whooping and yelling. My Mum thought it was ever so funny.

You might also try using the images as a springboard into developing surrealism in writing. Challenge the children to create surreal poems in which everyday objects become something unusual. You could imitate the following writing pattern and model a class version before the children write their own.

Walking in the park I saw –
an autumn tree burst into flames,
a cloud become a swan,
a bench grow crocodile's feet,
the children's slide stretch into a rainbow,
grass grow tongues and whisper secrets,
a statue wave its stony hands,
the boating pond turn into glass
and shatter into a thousand slices of ice...

As you approach the end of the **Investigation Phase**, remember to work with the class to **summarise** what has been learned, i.e. *what is the story really about?* One Year 6 class I worked with offered the following ideas: *happiness*; *relationships*; *that money doesn't make you happy*; *making friends*; *that the dogs are the happiest*; *posh people and snobs*; *things are not what they seem*. Ask the children to find a line or image of the text that captures the key meaning to the story, e.g. *You've got to have a bit of hope*. Or children could write a short **evaluation** of the book, possibly comparing it to other picture books they have read. They may find the following sentence starters helpful:

- *I like this book because...*
- *It made me think about...*
- *When I read the book, I felt...*
- *This book is about...*
- *The main point the author is making is...*
- *In comparison to other picture books such as... this book...*

At the end of the **Investigation Phase**, ensure that there is opportunity for the children to read and/or perform parts of the story so that they can demonstrate their understanding through **reading fluently**. The children could:

- present the text orally in groups of four, each taking the different voices;
- dramatise the text and present the story to other classes as a mini play in four parts.

Phase 3 – Independent understanding

When considering independent understanding, ask yourself the questions below.

- *Can children demonstrate understanding through talking or writing as a reader about the core text?*
- *Can children demonstrate understanding through identifying the key focus in another text and responding?*
- *Can children demonstrate understanding through applying what they have learned in their own writing?*

The Independent Understanding Phase

Demonstrate understanding through:

- talking or writing as a reader about the core text; or
- identifying the key focus in another text and responding; or
- applying what they have learned in their own writing.

Remember to revisit your **unit synopsis** and reflect on what the children have learned. Use this synopsis to guide how they will demonstrate understanding of the objectives that were identified in it:

- discuss how the author presents different viewpoints of similar experiences;
- talk about how the author uses illustrations to create an impact on the reader;
- empathise with the characters and talk or write in role.

You may like to brainstorm ideas around each of these bullet points to identify opportunities for children to demonstrate what they have learned. Here are some examples of what you could do.

Demonstrate understanding through talking or writing as a reader about the core text

There will be plenty of evidence from their writing and discussions about the story to demonstrate how well the children have understood it. For example, children could now write in role as Anthony Browne, explaining his authorial and artistic choices.

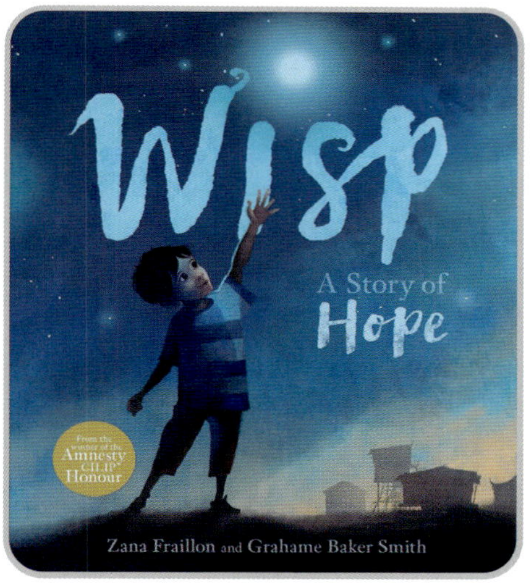

Demonstrate understanding through identifying the key focus in another text and responding

Provide children with a new text, such as *Wisp* by Zana Fraillon and Grahame Baker Smith. Spend time exploring the book with the children, this may include reading it to them and holding initial discussions in order to help them make the connections to the key focus areas for *Voices in the Park*. Children could then write about two of the characters, exploring what they are like and how they view the world and each other differently. Alternatively, they could talk or write discursively about how the illustrations create an impact on the reader, or write a response to part of the story as a character in role.

Demonstrate understanding through applying what they have learned in their own writing

Where children have developed a strong understanding of the structure and effect of the writing, they may be able to have a go at writing in the style of the author. On the next page is an example of a Year 6 child's independent story writing where they have explored the concept of viewpoint through their own version of *Beauty and the Beast*. Like *Voices in the Park*, the story is told through different voices and viewpoints – Belle, Beast, Gaston, the mob and Lumière.

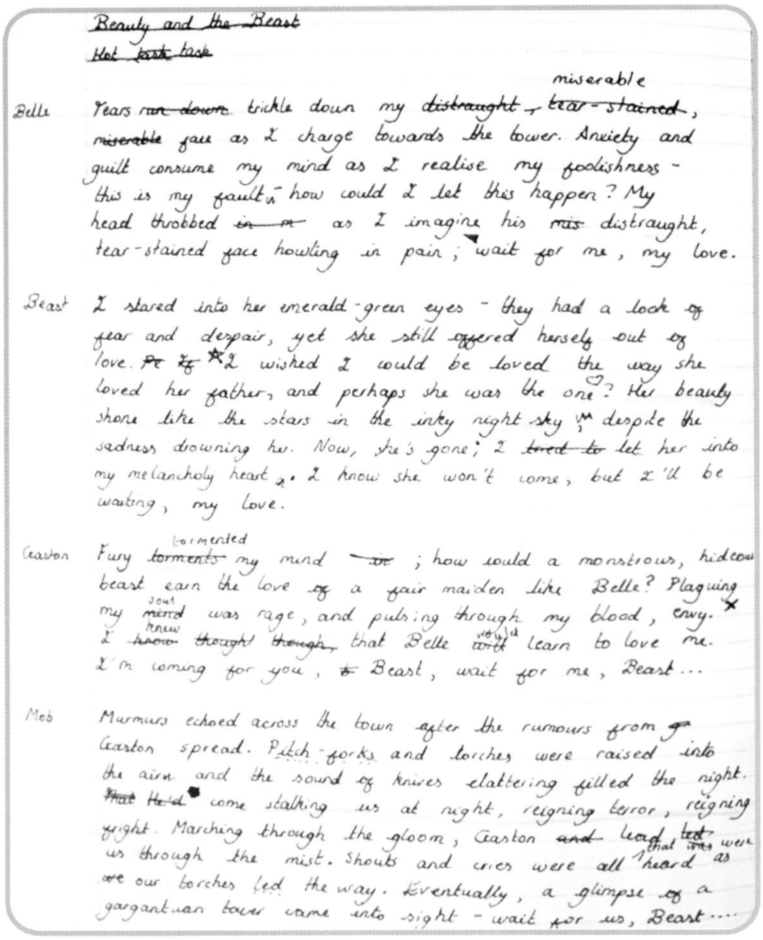

Beauty and the Beast
Hot ~~task~~ task

Belle — Tears ~~run down~~ trickle down my ~~distraught~~, ~~tear-stained~~ miserable, ~~miserable~~ face as I charge towards the tower. Anxiety and guilt consume my mind as I realise my foolishness - this is my fault; how could I let this happen? My head throbbed ~~in m~~ as I imagine his ~~mis~~ distraught, tear-stained face howling in pain; wait for me, my love.

Beast — I stared into her emerald-green eyes - they had a look of fear and despair, yet she still offered herself out of love. ~~Pe~~ ~~If~~ I wished I could be loved the way she loved her father, and perhaps she was the one? Her beauty shone like the stars in the inky night sky despite the sadness drowning her. Now, she's gone; I ~~tried to~~ let her into my melancholy heart. I know she won't come, but I'll be waiting, my love.

Gaston — Fury ~~torments~~ tormented my mind ~~or~~; how could a monstrous, hideous beast earn the love of a fair maiden like Belle? Plaguing my ~~mind~~ soul was rage, and pulsing through my blood, envy. I ~~know~~ ~~thought~~ ~~though~~ knew that Belle ~~will~~ would learn to love me. I'm coming for you, ~~B~~ Beast, wait for me, Beast...

Mob — Murmurs echoed across the town after the rumours from ~~G~~ Gaston spread. Pitch-forks and torches were raised into the air and the sound of knives clattering filled the night. ~~That Held~~ come stalking us at night, reigning terror, reigning fright. Marching through the gloom, Gaston ~~and~~ lead ~~led~~ us through the mist. Shouts and cries were all heard as ~~we~~ our torches led the way. Eventually, a glimpse of a gargantuan tower came into sight - wait for us, Beast...

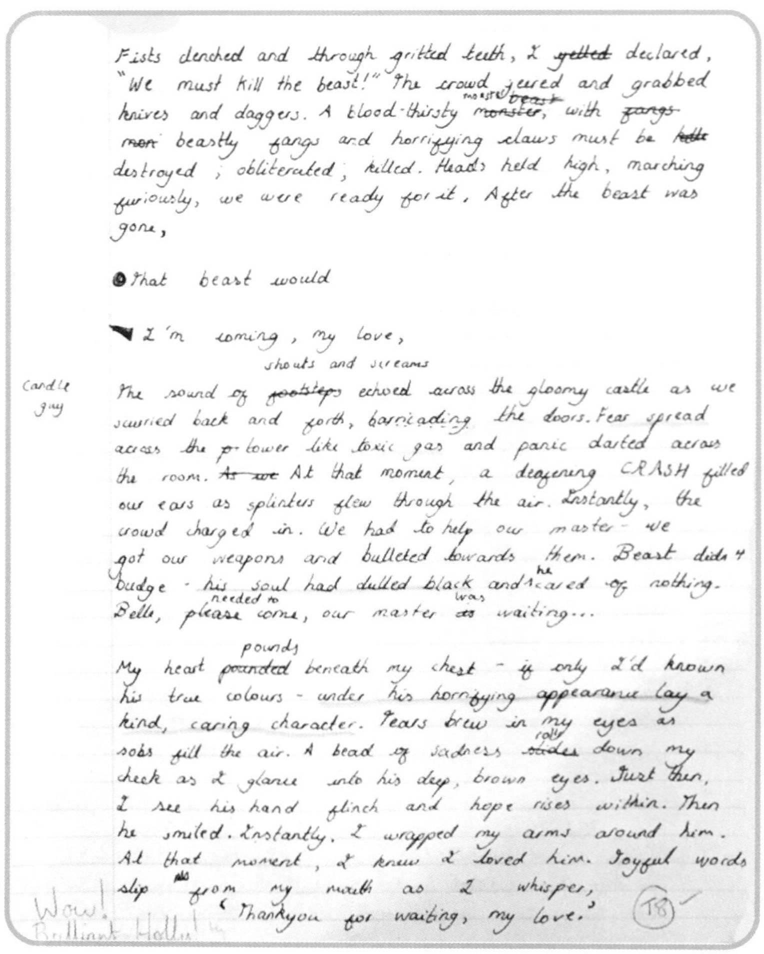

Fists clenched and through gritted teeth, I ~~yelled~~ declared, "We must kill the beast!" The crowd jeered and grabbed knives and daggers. A blood-thirsty ~~monster~~, ~~beast~~ monster with ~~fangs~~ ~~mon~~ beastly fangs and horrifying claws must be ~~kill~~ destroyed, obliterated, killed. Heads held high, marching furiously, we were ready for it. After the beast was gone,

That beast would

I'm coming, my love,

Candle guy — The sound of ~~footsteps~~ shouts and screams echoed across the gloomy castle as we scurried back and forth, barricading the doors. Fear spread across the ~~p~~ tower like toxic gas and panic darted across the room. ~~As we~~ At that moment, a deafening CRASH filled our ears as splinters flew through the air. Instantly, the crowd charged in. We had to help our master - we got our weapons and bulleted towards them. Beast didn't budge - his soul had dulled black and he scared of nothing. Belle, ~~please~~ needed to come, our master ~~is~~ was waiting...

My heart ~~pounded~~ pounds beneath my chest - if only I'd known his true colours - under his horrifying appearance lay a kind, caring character. Tears brew in my eyes as sobs fill the air. A bead of sadness ~~slides~~ rolls down my cheek as I glance into his deep, brown eyes. Just then, I see his hand flinch and hope rises within. Then he smiled. Instantly, I wrapped my arms around him. At that moment, I knew I loved him. Joyful words slip ~~as~~ from my mouth as I whisper, 'Thankyou for waiting, my love.'

Wow! Brilliant Holly!

2. *Overheard on a Saltmarsh* by Harold Monro

Background context notes

Harold Monro was an English poet who was born in Brussels, Belgium. He was most famous for owning The Poetry Bookshop in London, where he helped many up-and-coming poets to bring their work before the general public. *Overheard on a Saltmarsh* is arguably Harold Monro's best-known poem and quickly became a firm favourite of school poetry anthologies. This came as a surprise to Monro, who had not intended it for children. It depicts a conversation between two mythical characters, but also hints at an additional presence.

The initial brainstorm around literacy concepts

Role of characters/issues/information (as applicable)

There are clearly two characters in the poem: the nymph and the goblin. Children should be given the opportunity to explore each character's personality and behaviours. Comparing and contrasting the two characters would be a key discussion. This will also help them to perform the poem with meaning. The title of the poem hints at a third 'character' – whoever overheard the discussion. Time should be taken to explore this additional character and consider the significance of the discussion being overheard.

Role of setting/mood/tone (as applicable)

Given the title, it is important to explore the setting and consider the significance of this. Children may not have ever seen or heard of a salt marsh, so immersion in this through visualisation or experience will be essential. Children may like to think about whether the poem would change in meaning or significance if set somewhere else. *How central is the setting to the overall purpose of the poem?*

Structure of text – how the text works

The text is a poem that explores a conversation between two characters: the nymph and the goblin. Children need to be able to identify the different characters in order to build an impression of each.

Use of language, including figurative language

Both characters have a very distinctive spoken voice. Time should be spent looking at performance to assist the children in bringing these characters alive. The imagery developed around the beads enhances the goblin's desire for them. These lines need to be explored to help the children understand what the goblin does and why.

Perspectives/viewpoints – author/narrator/character/reader

Whilst children may be at the concrete stage of appreciating their own perspective of the poem, they would benefit from exploring how different characters behave and why this is. Using drama and performance will be a supportive way into this consideration.

Main themes/ideas/arguments

Underpinning the poem are the themes of desire and jealousy. Children should be given time to consider these and use their own vocabulary to express these feelings (such as *'really wanted'* or *'wanted something that someone else had'* etc.) Once they understand these themes, they should then reflect on how they fuel the way the characters act. Connections could be made with other texts that replicate the themes explored.

As you can see, the initial brainstorming opens up the vast potential of the poem. Before exploring the poem with the children, clarify what you want the children to have learned by the end of the unit. This will involve deciding which of the literary concepts will be the main focus. Having done this, craft your unit synopsis.

The unit synopsis

By the end of the unit, children may be able to:

- talk about different characters and their personalities in a text;
- compare and contrast characters and justify their opinions by making references to the text;
- talk about what motivates a character and how this may impact their behaviour.

Phase 1 – Introduction to the text

Hook the children's interest by presenting them with some green glass beads to hold and explore. Generate some initial language around the beads, identifying their beauty and value.

The Introduction Phase

Achieve basic understanding:

Before reading

- hook;
- context;
- activate prior knowledge.

While reading

- teacher models reading with fluency;
- prediction;
- initial responses;
- re-reading;
- initial vocabulary;
- literal retrieval;
- establish focus.

Support the children by exploring the **context** of the poem. You may like to show them some visual images to **activate their prior knowledge**, as well as supporting their initial understanding of the salt marsh, the nymph and the goblin (see the pictures below).

Model reading the poem to the children, focusing on expression and intonation. Use different 'voices' to represent each character in the poem.

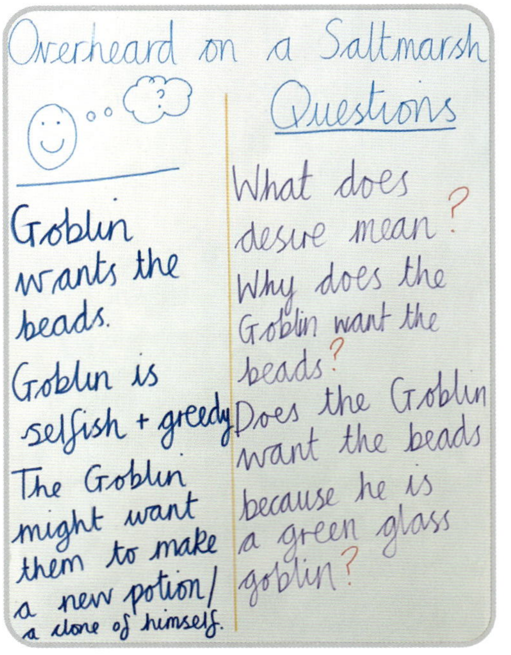

At the end of the poem, ask the children what they think has happened. *Which characters have they met in the poem?* Gather some **initial responses** with the class. In the example shown, the class teacher has captured some initial thoughts linked to what the Year 2 children thought and what questions they had that remained unanswered. This line of enquiry promotes genuine intrigue and exploration into the text. It is important that there is no perceived right or wrong – all ideas should be welcomed and captured through the shared discussion.

Re-read the poem, pausing to discuss any unfamiliar **vocabulary**. Support children with visual aids and child-friendly definitions to clarify meaning. You might like to embed the initial understanding of the poem through art. You could paint the scene, the characters or make green beads. Encourage children to **retrieve** words and phrases from the text to support their artistic choices.

Phase 2 – Investigation of the text

Deepen the children's understanding of the text by exploring some of the literary concepts related to it. You may like to open this up by asking them what is at the heart of this text and what it is really about. Through **oral comprehension**, explore various lines of enquiry, teaching children how to listen and respond as readers. They may benefit from some sentence stems that encourage tentative exploration, such as the ones listed below.

> **The Investigation Phase**
>
> Deepen understanding of the focus through:
>
> - oral comprehension;
> - strategic reading;
> - response activities;
> - exploring structure and effect;
> - summarising;
> - evaluating;
> - reading fluently.

- *It reminds me of…*
- *I'm not sure but…*
- *We think that…*
- *Perhaps,…*

Encourage discussion around the text, pausing to raise questions, re-read and clarify thinking. You may like to begin to **summarise** some of the key learning points with the children as you go on the flipchart.

Depending on your line of enquiry, pause and pose questions that will challenge thinking. Link this back to the unit synopsis where relevant. For example, one of the objectives was: *"By the end of the unit, children will be able to talk about different characters in a text. They will be able to compare and contrast characters and justify their opinions by making reference to the text."*

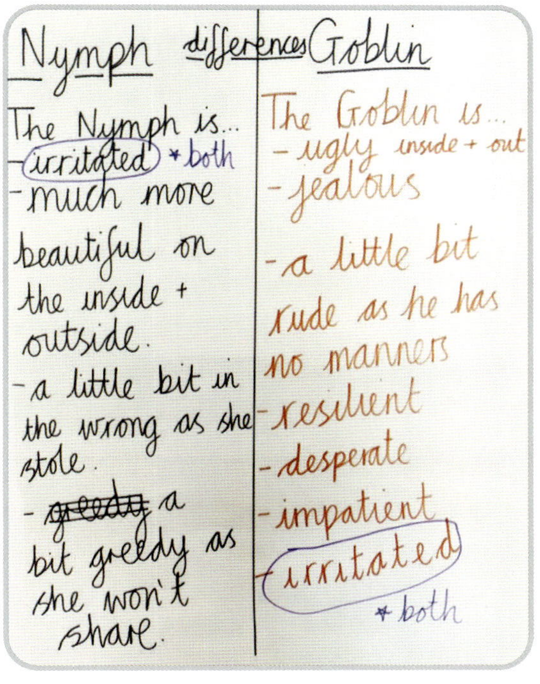

In the example depicted, the class had started to generate and bank ideas about the nymph and the goblin. You may like to use simple questions to generate discussion, such as: *what can you tell me about the two characters we have met in the poem?* Allow time for children to offer suggestions and collectively form a shared response. In order to explore the characters in this way, children will need to revisit the text and justify their opinions.

Once the brainstorming has taken place, you could demonstrate how to write an explanatory **response** to the text. This will be reliant on key sentence stems that support the structure of a written response.

Here is an example, with the sentence stems underlined.

> *<u>I think that</u> the goblin is a very greedy character. I <u>know this because</u> he keeps telling the nymph to give them to him. <u>He also says that</u> he desires them. <u>This shows that</u> he is only thinking about himself.*

The children could then have a go at writing their own answer, using the scaffold to discuss the other character/s in the poem.

As children begin to form opinions about the characters, it is important that they are given the opportunity to **respond** and explore the poem through drama. Initially, you or a child could be in role as one of the characters, with the rest of the class asking questions to help them understand the character's motives and actions. In pairs, children could then act out the conversation between the nymph and goblin, either using the poem as a script, or retelling the events through their own words. You could also challenge the children to act in role as eyewitnesses to the scene and ask them what they heard and saw, or how the characters were acting at the salt marsh.

Where themes are uncovered, such as the topic of jealousy seen in the example, pause to clarify meaning. This is a great opportunity to find connections to wider reading, drawing in characters from other books that are familiar to the children. Again, all of this links to the unit objectives: *"Children will also be able to talk about what motivates a character and how this may impact their behaviour."*

In addition to the discussions around some of the themes explored in the text, you may like to help the children to write in the style of the author, **exploring the poem's structure and effect**. You could use a scaffold or writing frame to support the children in their task (see example).

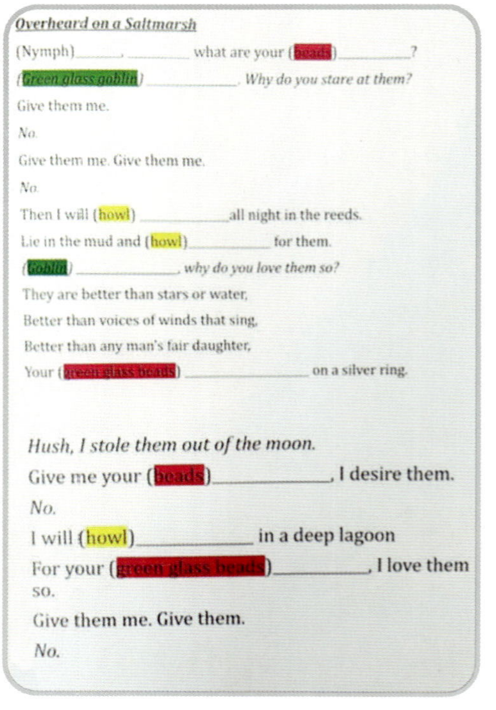

Overheard on a Saltmarsh

(Nymph)______, ________ what are your (beads) ________?

(Green glass goblin) __________. *Why do you stare at them?*

Give them me.

No.

Give them me. Give them me.

No.

Then I will (howl) __________ all night in the reeds.

Lie in the mud and (howl) _________ for them.

(Goblin) __________, *why do you love them so?*

They are better than stars or water,

Better than voices of winds that sing,

Better than any man's fair daughter,

Your (green glass beads) ____________ on a silver ring.

Hush, I stole them out of the moon.

Give me your (beads) __________, I desire them.

No.

I will (howl) __________ in a deep lagoon

For your (green glass beads) ________, I love them so.

Give them me. Give them.

No.

Once the children have had a go at writing in the style of the author, ensure that there is time for them to read and perform their innovations. Discuss the choices they made and explore the themes that lie at the heart of the new poems. See **video clip 18** for a Year 2 child reading their innovated poem.

By the end of the **Investigation Phase**, children should be able to demonstrate a rich understanding of the text by **reading it fluently**. Rehearse reading the poem as a class, exploring intonation and expression that clarifies meaning. You may like to initially encourage the children to imitate your own reading, copying your voice and expression. Children may also benefit from marking the text to identify where you add emphasis to words, or where you change the pitch or volume.

Having practised reading the text, consider how children could perform it. This could be through dance, with groups of children putting movement to gentle music. Alternatively, children could work in small groups to rehearse a choral performance, deciding how they should use their voice to demonstrate the characters and their emotions.

Support the children through their oral performance of the poem. You could create a map for the text to provide a visual aid that supports internalisation of the words or phrasing.

In **video clips 19 & 20**, children in Reception and Year 2 demonstrate their understanding of Harold Monro's *Overheard on a Saltmarsh* through performance of the poem.

Phase 3 – Independent understanding

When considering independent understanding, ask yourself the questions below.

> **The Independent Understanding Phase**
>
> Demonstrate understanding through:
>
> - talking or writing as a reader about the core text; or
> - identifying the key focus in another text and responding; or
> - applying what they have learned in their own writing.

- *Can children demonstrate understanding through talking or writing as a reader about the core text?*
- *Can children demonstrate understanding through identifying the key focus in another text and responding?*
- *Can children demonstrate understanding through applying what they have learned in their own writing?*

Remember to revisit your **unit synopsis** and reflect on what the children have learned. Use this synopsis to guide how they will demonstrate understanding of the objectives that were identified in it:

- talk about different characters and their personalities in a text;
- compare and contrast characters and justify their opinions by making references to the text;
- talk about what motivates a character and how this may impact their behaviour.

You may like to brainstorm ideas around each of these bullet points to identify opportunities for students to demonstrate what they have learned. Here are some examples of what you could do.

Demonstrate understanding through talking or writing as a reader about the core text

In the examples on the next page, the Year 2 children were asked to write in role as either the nymph or the goblin, showcasing their personality and characteristics.

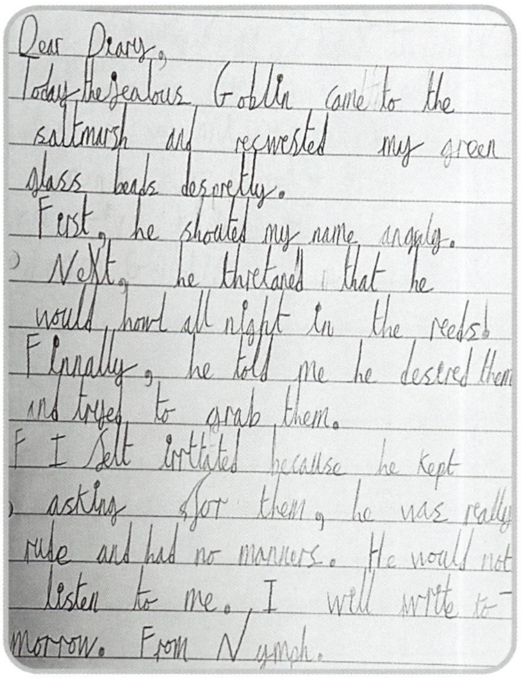
Dear Diary,
Today the Jealous Goblin came to the saltmarsh and reqwested my green glass beads desperetly.
Ferst, he shouted my name angrily.
Next, he thretaned that he would howl all night in the reeds.
Finally, he told me he desired them and tryed to grab them.
I felt irritated because he kept asking for them, he was really rude and had no manners. He would not listen to me. I will write to-morrow. From Nymph.

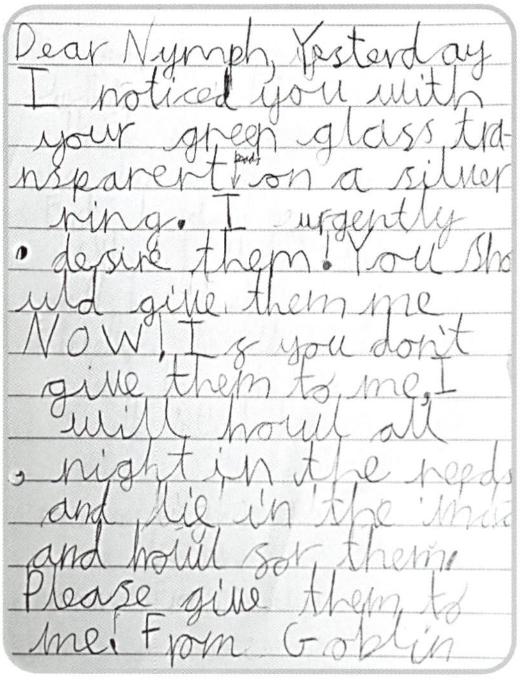
Dear Nymph, Yesterday I noticed you with your green glass transparent beads on a silver ring. I urgently desire them! You should give them me NOW! If you don't give them to me, I will howl all night in the reeds and lie in the mud and howl for them. Please give them to me! From Goblin

Demonstrate understanding through identifying the key focus in another text and responding

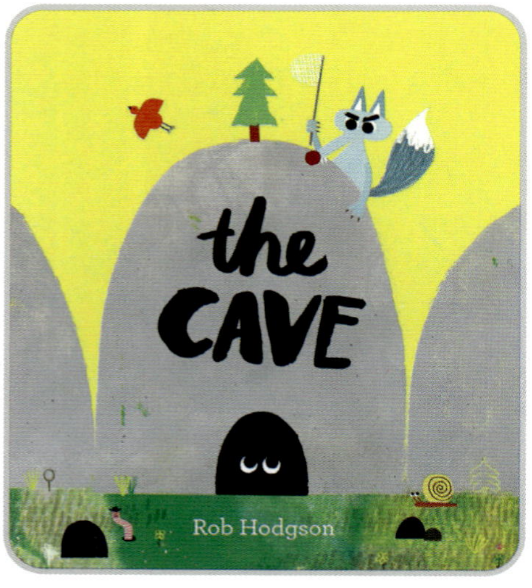

Choose another poem or picture book that explores contrasting characters which the children could talk about, using the knowledge that they have gained from investigating *Overheard on a Saltmarsh*. For example, in *The Cave* by Rob Hodgson, *what does the wolf want? What do we think his motivations are? How does his behaviour change at the end of the book?*

Demonstrate understanding through applying what they have learned in their own writing

Where children have developed a strong understanding of the structure and effect of the writing, they may be able to have a go at writing in the style of the poet. This could be using a scaffold, as demonstrated in the **Investigation Phase**, or by writing a short narrative of their own that explores similar themes and characters.

Our thanks to Nicole Piper and her Year 2 class at Warren Road Primary School for the worked examples.

3. *Fox* by Margaret Wild and Ron Brooks

Background context notes

Margaret Wild is one of Australia's most highly respected picture-book creators. She has been awarded the Nan Chauncy Award and the Lady Cutler Award for her contributions to Australian children's literature. Wild is known for taking inspiration from her own life experiences, and those that she encounters in the world around her. *Fox*, illustrated by Ron Brooks, captures the colours of the Australian landscape and is a powerful story about trust and betrayal.

The initial brainstorm around literacy concepts

Role of characters/issues/information (as applicable)

Different relationships are explored in this text. A friendship exists between Magpie and Dog, but Magpie's desire to fly sees her form a relationship with untrustworthy Fox. This ultimately leads Magpie to unfortunate circumstances where she is forced to reflect on her loyalty to Dog. The descriptions of Fox are closely linked to fire, *"...rich red coat. He flickers through the trees like a tongue of fire"; "Fox scorches through woodlands...".* There is a comparison being made between Fox and the bushfire that took Magpie's ability to fly away from her. Dog rescues Magpie at the beginning of the story from the remnants of the bushfire. He again rescues Magpie at the end of the story when her loyalty to Dog encourages her to not give up.

Role of setting/mood/tone (as applicable)

The language depicting the settings powerfully establishes the mood. The story begins with descriptions to infer the negative aftermath of a bushfire. The story ends with Magpie abandoned in a desert, described as *"hot and red"*, another reference to the bushfire with Magpie feeling *"...herself burning into nothingness."* The setting is specifically Australian with mention of Australian flora and landscapes.

Structure of text – how the text works

It is written in a narrative style, reminiscent of either a wishing or losing tale. The story is told through both the words and the images. In fact, the text is often incorporated into the scene, or presented both horizontally and vertically, rather like a scrap book. The layout of the narrative encourages deeper exploration into the images themselves as you have to orientate the book.

Use of language, including figurative language

Colours are referred to as reflections of the character's emotions. Describing Magpie's despair, Wild writes, *"…she feels herself melting into blackness… into the shadows of the rocks."* Conversely, when Magpie is feeling elated, she says, *"… races… into the blueness"*. The metaphors *"melting into blackness"* and *"burning into nothingness"* are used at the beginning and end of the story to depict Magpie's feelings. The speech verbs chosen convey character emotion, as well as what the characters say and their actions. The author cleverly describes Fox's personality traits through Magpie's senses, *"And at night his smell seems to fill the cave – a smell of range and envy and loneliness."* The text is full of rich language that has instructional potential to enhance children's vocabulary.

Perspectives/viewpoints – author/narrator/character/reader

It is easy to view Fox as a negative character, given his actions and descriptions. Children could also consider the actions of Magpie and her loyalty towards Dog at different stages of the text.

Main themes/ideas/arguments

Underpinning the story are themes of friendship and loyalty. Other themes that could also be explored include risk and betrayal.

As you can see, the initial brainstorming opens up the vast potential of the book. Before exploring the story with the children, clarify what you want the children to have learned by the end of the unit. This will involve deciding which of the literary concepts will be the main focus. Having done this, craft your unit synopsis.

The unit synopsis

By the end of the unit, children may be able to:

- identify the theme of loyalty in other texts;
- discuss how authors describe a character's emotions through the setting;
- mirror the language used to describe the characters' movements in their own writing.

Phase 1 – Introduction to the text

Hook children by allowing them to explore items collected from a bushfire, such as burnt leaves, a burnt magpie feather, ash, etc. Provide context and background information about how wildlife is affected by bushfires. **Activate prior knowledge** by asking 'tuning in' questions to engage thinking, such as, *what happens to wildlife in bushfires? What happens to the animals' homes?*

> **The Introduction Phase**
>
> Achieve basic understanding:
>
> **Before reading**
> - hook;
> - context;
> - activate prior knowledge.
>
> **While reading**
> - teacher models reading with fluency;
> - prediction;
> - initial responses;
> - re-reading;
> - initial vocabulary;
> - literal retrieval;
> - establish focus.

You may like to tap into children's experiences by naming emotions and considering how they can be represented by colours. Use a colour wheel and label emotions on the different colours.

Model reading the story to the children with **fluency**, focusing on expression matched to the mood of the text. Read dialogue the way in which it is written, with reference to punctuation and speech verbs. Pause at relevant points to ask prediction questions, such as: *where is Fox taking Magpie? Will Magpie make the journey back home? Do you think Dog is worried about Magpie?* Begin to ask **literal retrieval** questions so the class begin to build a basic understanding of the text. For example, *where does Dog take Magpie?*

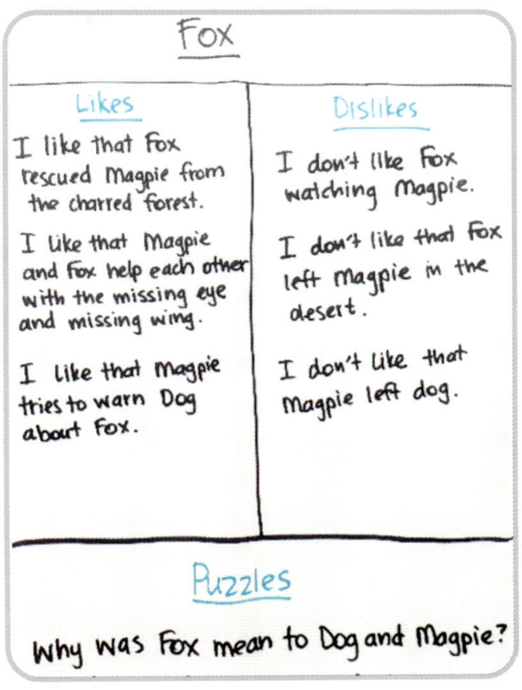

At the conclusion of the first read-through, gather **initial responses** on the flipchart (see image). *What did the children like about the story? What did they dislike? What were some puzzles that were left unanswered?* Encourage them to provide answers that are responsive to the text, rather than personal opinions about what they like and dislike. Be prepared to add children's questions that can be returned to as the text is **re-read** and their understanding deepens.

During **re-reading** of the text, ask children to echo your expression and intonation and then join in with a choral reading of the text. This could be practised in small groups or pairs. Explicitly teach value-adding vocabulary from the text in every lesson, providing child-friendly definitions with an expectation that the children use the vocabulary in context. Link word meanings to understanding the text.

Phase 2 – Investigation of the text

Once children have grasped a literal understanding of the text, begin to develop deeper understanding linked to the literacy concepts. Through **oral comprehension** and **response activities**, develop children as **strategic readers**. Encourage them to go back and re-read, pause for clarity, and raise questions.

The Investigation Phase

Deepen understanding of the focus through:

- oral comprehension;
- strategic reading;
- response activities;
- exploring structure and effect;
- summarising;
- evaluating;
- reading fluently.

During the **Investigation Phase**, children could deepen their understanding of the concept of 'loyalty', as demonstrated by the actions of the characters. You may like to use a graphic organiser to locate evidence from the text to support the question: *who is Magpie loyal to?*

Who is Magpie loyal to?	
DOG	***FOX***
Magpie says to Dog, "I will be your missing eye, and you will be my wings."	*Magpie trembles and shrinks away when she sees Fox.*
Magpie tries to warn Dog about Fox.	*Magpie leaves with Fox whilst Dog is sleeping.*
Magpie says the following, to Fox (twice), "I will never leave Dog. I am his missing eye, and he is my missing wings."	
Magpie thinks of Dog waking to find her gone and begins the journey home back to Dog.	

Children could respond to the characters' actions and think about the way their feelings are inferred through the text. Model thinking aloud as a reader, slowing things down and describing what you think is occurring. For example:

> *"It says in the text that Magpie huddles. She must be feeling unsafe or worried because that's how people are feeling when they huddle [demonstrate what huddling looks like]. A scruff of feathers adrift in the heat. Adrift means to float. A magpie can't float. I think the author has said adrift because it makes it sound like the heat is all around her – over her, under her. A scruff of feathers implied that she's weak, just a pile of feathers that are scruffy. There's not much to her."*

Select sections to read closely by reading the text bit-by-bit, asking children questions and providing ample exploration and investigation time. Lead discussions and prompt the class to delve deeper to form understandings. Encourage all responses. Model and guide the use of sentence stems that encourage exploration of the text in a 'safe' environment, where answers are provided tentatively to allow for changing of minds.

- *I wonder if...*
- *I may be incorrect in saying this but...*
- *I'd like to add to what Jim said and say...*

It's also useful to model sentence stems that give children a structured way of **summarising** their thoughts and providing extended answers to inferential questions, such as *Point*, *Evidence*, *Explain*. This is demonstrated below for the question: *how is Magpie feeling?*

Point: *The author suggests that Magpie is heartbroken.*

Evidence: *In the text it states that Magpie drags her body into the shadows. Furthermore, she whispers, "I will never again be able to fly."*

Explain: *It is clear that Magpie is heartbroken. She is whispering and dragging her body which are natural responses to being deeply upset.*

Children could also explore the author's use of figurative language, colour, and setting, and how these connect with the characters' emotions. You may like to provide the children with key emotions and ask them to find evidence in the text that exemplify these.

The table below shows children's ideas (***in bold and italics***) using quotes from the book to support their opinions.

helpless	***Magpie does not want his help.*** *"I will never again be able to fly."* *"How would you feel if you couldn't run?"*
frustrated	*"An eye is nothing!"*
depressed	***Magpie drags her body into the shadows of the rocks, until she feels herself melting into blackness.*** ***Sighing, Magpie does as he asks.***
heartbroken	***She wakes with a rush of grief.***

At the end of the **Investigation Phase**, ensure that there is an opportunity for the students to read and/or perform the text so that they can demonstrate their understanding through reading fluently.

Phase 3 – Independent understanding

When considering independent understanding, ask yourself the questions below.

> **The Independent Understanding Phase**
>
> Demonstrate understanding through:
>
> - talking or writing as a reader about the core text; or
> - identifying the key focus in another text and responding; or
> - applying what they have learned in their own writing.

- *Can children demonstrate understanding through talking or writing as a reader about the core text?*
- *Can children demonstrate understanding through identifying the key focus in another text and responding?*
- *Can children demonstrate understanding through applying what they have learned in their own writing?*

Remember to revisit your **unit synopsis** and reflect on what the children have learned. Use this synopsis to guide how they will demonstrate understanding of the objectives that were identified in it:

- identify the theme of loyalty in other texts;

- discuss how authors describe a character's emotions through setting;
- mirror the language used to describe the characters' movements in their own writing.

You may like to brainstorm ideas around each of these bullet points to identify opportunities for students to demonstrate what they have learned. Below are some examples of what you could do.

Demonstrate understanding through talking or writing as a reader about the core text

Children could write in role as the author Margaret Wild, describing how she sewed the theme of loyalty through the text.

Demonstrate understanding through identifying the key focus in another text and responding

The Tale of Desperaux by Kate DiCamillo is a lovely story to read for pleasure alongside this Talk for Reading unit. After reading the text, revisit and examine Chapter 12. Ask children to consider the question: *who is Antoinette loyal to?* Children could locate text evidence and provide written answers to this. You can help scaffold the responses, by providing the sentence starters previously modelled to students, such as these listed below.

- *The author suggests that...*
- *In the text it states...*
- *It is clear that...*

Demonstrate understanding through applying what they have learned in their own writing

Revisit a simile from *Fox* and explore the author's deliberate use of language to show how a character moved. For example, *"He flickers through the trees like a tongue of fire, and Magpie trembles."*

Children could innovate on this sentence pattern and apply the use of similes and verbs to create an effect on the reader. You may like to provide a rich picture prompt, such as: https://www.onceuponapicture.co.uk/portfolio_page/dream-big/.

Our thanks to The Talk for Writing consultants at DSF, Australia for the planning and worked examples.

4. *Invictus* by William Ernest Henley

Background context notes

Invictus is a short poem by the British poet William Ernest Henley, first published in 1888. Henley wrote the poem while recovering in an infirmary, following an amputation of his left leg due to tuberculosis. The poem is known for its themes of willpower and strength, and has been quoted by numerous people, including Winston Churchill, Barack Obama and Nelson Mandela. Mandela, while incarcerated at Robben Island prison, recited the poem to fellow prisoners and told the world that he drew upon the words in his hours of greatest need.

The initial brainstorm around literacy concepts

Role of characters/issues/information (as applicable)

The poem is written in the first person, with the 'speaker' talking about the seemingly insurmountable challenges that they face in their life. By definition, *invictus* means 'unconquerable', and the poem explores the speaker's inner-belief and courage to overcome whatever barriers they are faced with.
The 'speaker' in the poem talks aloud, almost as a monologue, comforting themselves with their words of assurance and motivation. The poem explores significant issues that humans face, such as suffering, fate and free will.

Role of setting/mood/tone (as applicable)

It could be said that Henley uses the setting to mirror the character's mood. The start of the poem begins, *"Out of the night that covers me, / Black as the pit from pole to pole"*. The use of the night, darkness and the connection to the world begins to hint at the turmoil that the speaker is living through. Later, he refers to an afterlife that is filled with horror, but talks about being unafraid. The connection between the character's emotions, beliefs and the setting surrounding them has a significant impact on the meaning. Whilst the overall tone of the poem is fairly optimistic, the mood is dark. This may symbolize the role of the character, courageously fighting the hand that they have been dealt.

Structure of text – how the text works

Invictus consists of four stanzas, each consisting of four lines. Each stanza has an *abab* rhyme scheme and each line consists of eight syllables.

Use of language, including figurative language

The poem is rich in figurative language, beginning with the personification of *"the night"* that creates an air of menace, then giving *"circumstance"* human-like qualities. By using this technique, Henley captures the struggle between the speaker in the poem and the world that they are endlessly fighting. This atmosphere is further mirrored through the use of simile (*"Black as the pit"*) and metaphor (*"bludgeonings of chance"*). Additional devices, such as alliteration, can be seen in the lines: *"Under the bludgeonings of chance / My head is bloody, but unbowed."* This creates a harshness that resonates when reading the poem aloud, heightening the importance of the meaning in the words. Furthermore, the entire poem could be perceived as a metaphor about the state of the human condition.

Perspectives/viewpoints – author/narrator/character/reader

There are many perspectives that could be explored in the poem. Firstly, there is the perspective of the poet, Henley, who wrote the poem while he was recovering from a serious illness. Then there is the perspective of the voice or narrator of the poem, and the significance of the message they are portraying. There is also the perspective of the numerous readers of the poem who have been inspired by its meaning, such as Nelson Mandela during his time of need. An avenue of exploration might be to look at how different people might connect to and react to the poem.

Main themes/ideas/arguments

The title of the poem means *'unconquerable'* or *'undefeated'* in Latin. The poem explores the themes of free will, fate, resilience, suffering and perseverance. It looks at the concept of staying strong in the face of adversity.

As you can see, the initial brainstorming opens up the vast potential of the poem. Before exploring the poem with the children, clarify what you want the children to have learned by the end of the unit. This will involve deciding which of the literary concepts will be the main focus. Having done this, craft your unit synopsis.

The unit synopsis

By the end of the unit, children may be able to:

- talk about the themes of free will and fate in a range of literature;
- understand the significance that words can have on people's lives;
- appreciate how circumstance can shape a person's future.

Phase 1 – Introduction to the text

Hook the children in by looking at the title of the poem. Discuss the etymology of the word *invictus* and encourage children to make any links or associations with its meaning.

Model reading the poem to the children, focusing on your expression and intonation. Encourage children to jot down their **initial responses**. They could respond through drawing or writing down words and phrases, although they should be able to articulate their ideas. Discuss their first impressions as a class.

> **The Introduction Phase**
>
> Achieve basic understanding:
>
> **Before reading**
> - hook;
> - context;
> - activate prior knowledge.
>
> **While reading**
> - teacher models reading with fluency;
> - prediction;
> - initial responses;
> - re-reading;
> - initial vocabulary;
> - literal retrieval;
> - establish focus.

Read through the poem bit-by-bit, exploring the meaning of the **vocabulary** in **context**. Begin to draw on the children's knowledge of language and the connections to their own lives, supporting them in their initial understanding.

At this point, you may like to read about William Earnest Henley's life and discuss the key events that inspired the poem.

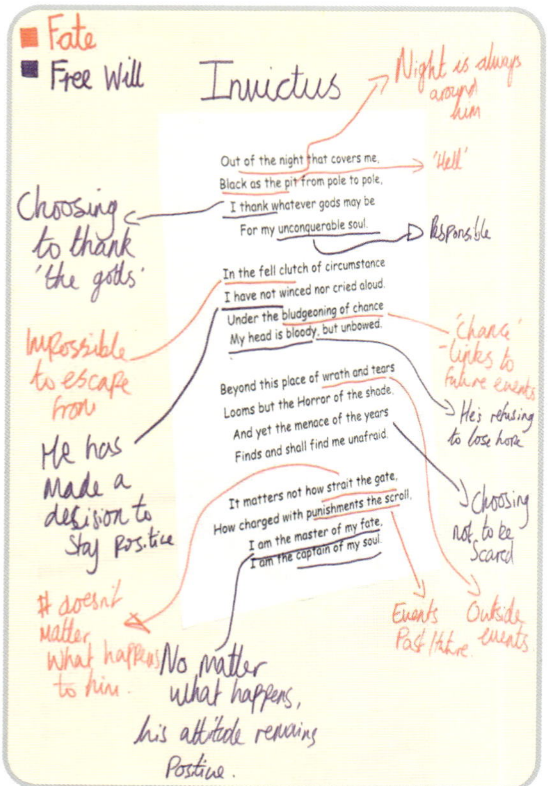

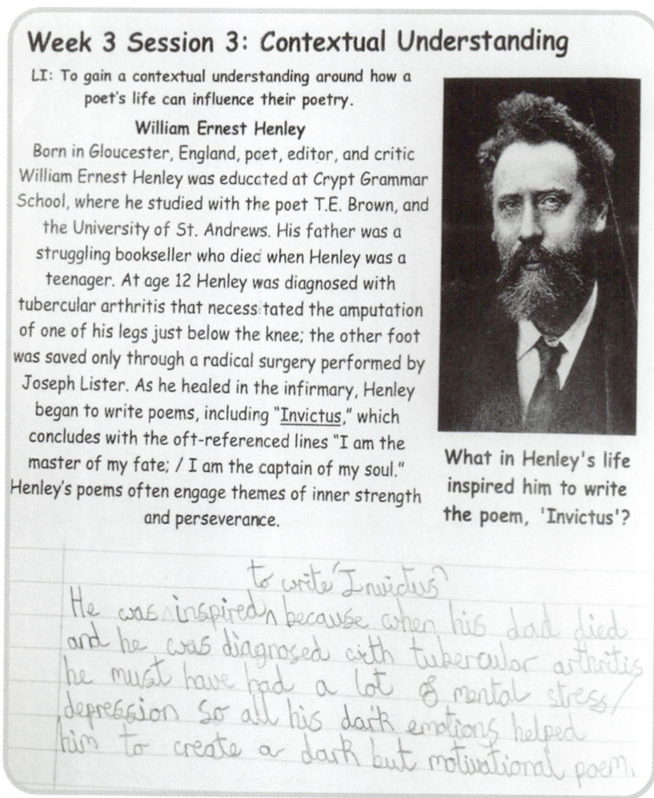
Week 3 Session 3: Contextual Understanding

LI: To gain a contextual understanding around how a poet's life can influence their poetry.

William Ernest Henley

Born in Gloucester, England, poet, editor, and critic William Ernest Henley was educated at Crypt Grammar School, where he studied with the poet T.E. Brown, and the University of St. Andrews. His father was a struggling bookseller who died when Henley was a teenager. At age 12 Henley was diagnosed with tubercular arthritis that necessitated the amputation of one of his legs just below the knee; the other foot was saved only through a radical surgery performed by Joseph Lister. As he healed in the infirmary, Henley began to write poems, including "Invictus," which concludes with the oft-referenced lines "I am the master of my fate; / I am the captain of my soul." Henley's poems often engage themes of inner strength and perseverance.

What in Henley's life inspired him to write the poem, 'Invictus'?

He was inspired to write 'Invictus' because when his dad died and he was diagnosed with tubercular arthritis he must have had a lot of mental stress/depression so all his dark emotions helped him to create a dark but motivational poem.

Re-read the poem a number of times with the class, encouraging them to join in and say the words aloud. Rehearse the poem with intonation, expression and fluency.

Establish the main focus for the **Investigation Phase** and draw up some key questions to explore.

- *How are the themes of free will and fate explored in literature?*
- *How can circumstance influence a character or a person's future?*

Phase 2 – Investigation of the text

Re-read the poem and, through **oral comprehension**, discuss the main ideas of each stanza. You may like to initially slow down the reading, allowing time to reflect on the literary concepts that lie at its heart. Spend time discussing the meaning of the poem with the class, pausing to reflect on the discussions as they unfold.

> **The Investigation Phase**
>
> Deepen understanding of the focus through:
>
> - oral comprehension;
> - strategic reading;
> - response activities;
> - exploring structure and effect;
> - summarising;
> - evaluating;
> - reading fluently.

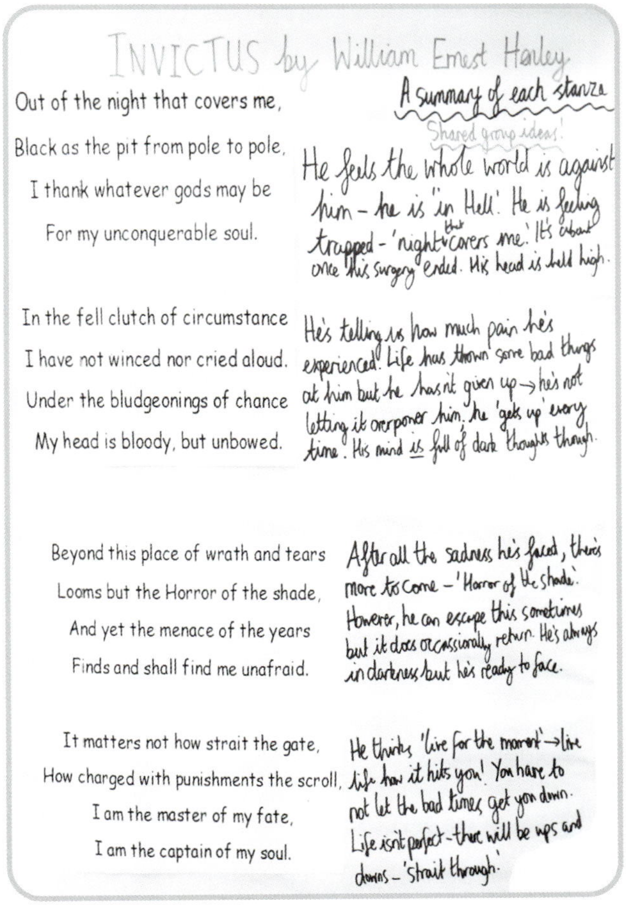

INVICTUS by William Ernest Henley

A summary of each stanza

Shared group ideas!

Out of the night that covers me, Black as the pit from pole to pole, I thank whatever gods may be For my unconquerable soul.	He feels the whole world is against him – he is 'in Hell'. He is feeling trapped – 'night that covers me.' It's about once this surgery ended. His head is held high.
In the fell clutch of circumstance I have not winced nor cried aloud. Under the bludgeonings of chance My head is bloody, but unbowed.	He's telling us how much pain he's experienced. Life has thrown some bad things at him but he hasn't given up → he's not letting it overpower him, he 'gets up' every time. His mind is full of dark thoughts though.
Beyond this place of wrath and tears Looms but the Horror of the shade, And yet the menace of the years Finds and shall find me unafraid.	After all the sadness he's faced, there's more to come – 'Horror of the shade'. However, he can escape this sometimes but it does occasionally return. He's always in darkness but he's ready to face.
It matters not how strait the gate, How charged with punishments the scroll, I am the master of my fate, I am the captain of my soul.	He thinks 'live for the moment' → live life how it hits you! You have to not let the bad times get you down. Life isn't perfect – there will be ups and downs – 'strait through'.

Children may like to jot down their thinking in a 'magpie' book as it develops. Following the discussions, model how to **summarise** the themes explored. This example shows the shared response, captured by the class teacher during the oral exploration of the text.

Plan for **response activities**, such as 'role-on-the-wall', pictured below. Explore which lines in the poem reveal the speaker's internal thoughts and feelings, compared to his external circumstance.

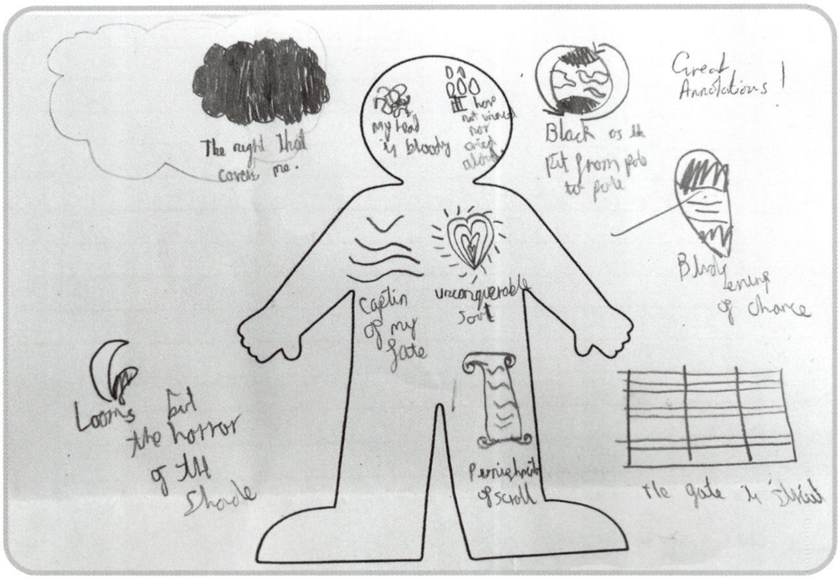

Model writing a short piece of 'Outside/Inside' shared writing using the ideas of *Invictus* as inspiration. For example:

> *Outside, the taunting of the night oppresses and covers all hope.*
> *Inside, my unconquerable soul remains unscathed.*

Discuss the words *'suffering'* and *'resilience'* and explore how these themes connect to the poem. In the example on the right, the child has followed on from the group discussion to develop their own opinion of these key themes, demonstrating their understanding at this stage. Notice how they have been taught to go back and make references to the text to support their opinions.

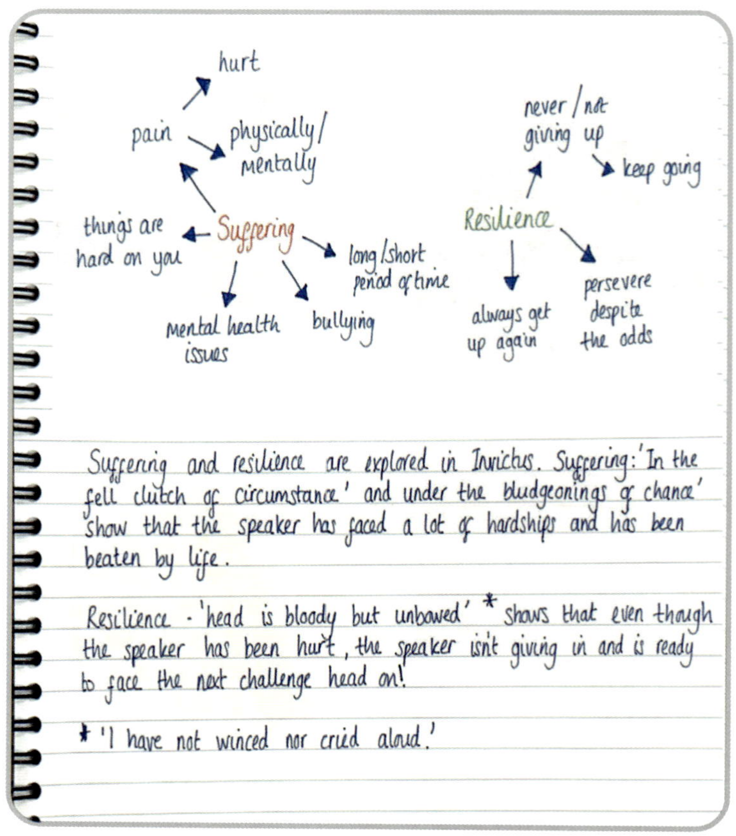

Revisit the first key question that was created at the end of the **Introduction Phase**: *how are the themes of free will and fate explored in the*

poem, Invictus? Look at the text again together, and engage the class in dialogic discussion about it, enabling them to collectively deepen their understanding. Form a shared response, **summarising** the learning.

Now look at the second key question: *how can circumstance influence a character or a person's future?* Building on the previous class discussions, you could link this to the two overarching themes of suffering and resilience. The child's writing below illustrates how they are beginning to **summarise** all of the relevant research that has preceded this task, in order to form a quality response. This shows how they are now reading strategically, drawing on their prior knowledge and discussion, in order to make sense of a highly challenging text.

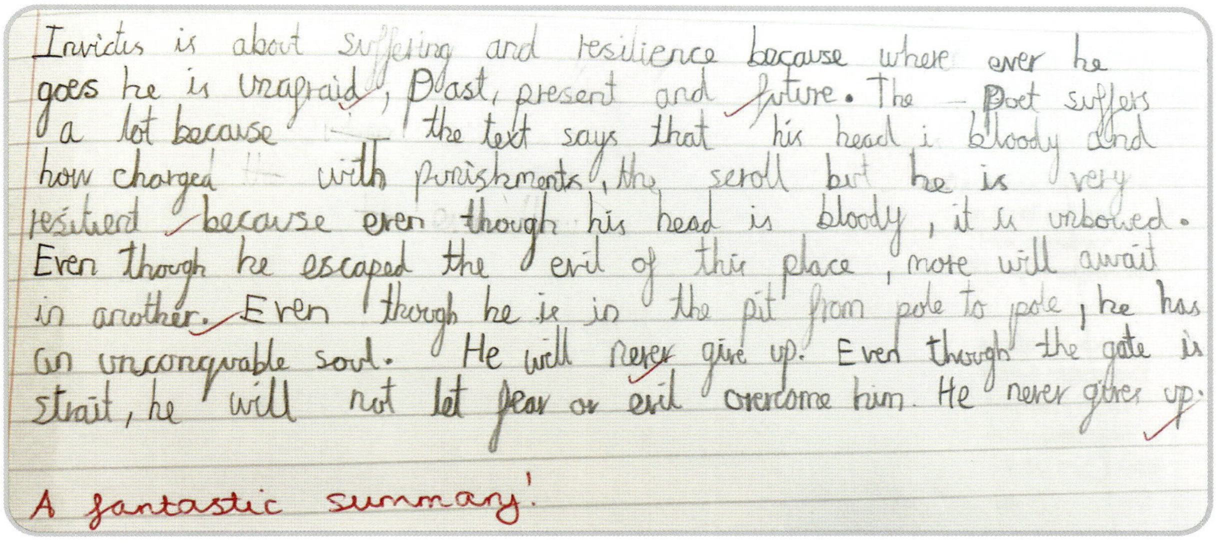
Invictus is about suffering and resilience because where ever he goes he is unafraid, past, present and future. The poet suffers a lot because the text says that his head is bloody and how charged with punishments, the scroll but he is very resilient because even though his head is bloody, it is unbowed. Even though he escaped the evil of this place, more will await in another. Even though he is in the pit from pole to pole, he has an unconquerable soul. He will never give up. Even though the gate is strait, he will not let fear or evil overcome him. He never gives up.

A fantastic summary!

Watch the interview with Morgan Freeman where he discusses how instrumental the poem *Invictus* was in Nelson Mandela's life https://www.youtube.com/watch?v=d3dZngCraqs&feature=emb_logo.

As a class, explore the following question: *why did Invictus give Nelson Mandela what he needed to keep going?* Form a shared response, **evaluating** the impact of the poem.

At the end of the **Investigation Phase**, ensure that there is an opportunity for the children to read and/or perform the poem so that they can demonstrate their understanding through reading fluently.

Phase 3 – Independent understanding

When considering independent understanding, ask yourself the questions below.

- *Can children demonstrate understanding through talking or writing as a reader about the core text?*
- *Can children demonstrate understanding through identifying the key focus in another text and responding?*
- *Can children demonstrate understanding through applying what they have learned in their own writing?*

The Independent Understanding Phase

Demonstrate understanding through:

- talking or writing as a reader about the core text; or
- identifying the key focus in another text and responding; or
- applying what they have learned in their own writing.

Remember to revisit your **unit synopsis** and reflect on what the children have learned. Use this synopsis to guide how they will demonstrate understanding of the objectives that were identified in it:

- talk about the themes of free will and fate in a range of literature;
- understand the significance that words can have on people's lives;
- appreciate how circumstance can shape a person's future.

You may like to brainstorm ideas around each of these bullet points to identify opportunities for children to demonstrate what they have learned. Here are some examples of what you could do.

Demonstrate understanding through talking or writing as a reader about the core text

Children could write in role as Nelson Mandela, explaining the impact that the poem *Invictus* had on his life and the courage that the words gave him.

Demonstrate understanding through identifying the key focus in another text and responding

The following examples are linked to *Macbeth: A Shakespeare Story* by Andrew Matthews. This was the class book used as part of their daily read-aloud programme.

Facilitate a discussion with the class about how the themes of free will and fate are explored in *Macbeth.* Brainstorm initial responses and collect them on the flipchart. Children could then write a short discursive response based on the prompt:

Mandela was a servant to free will. Macbeth was a servant to fate. Discuss.

In the example below, the child demonstrates not only their understanding of free will and fate, but also their understanding of how characters in fiction, through history and in the present day, overcome difficulties in order to better their lives or those of others.

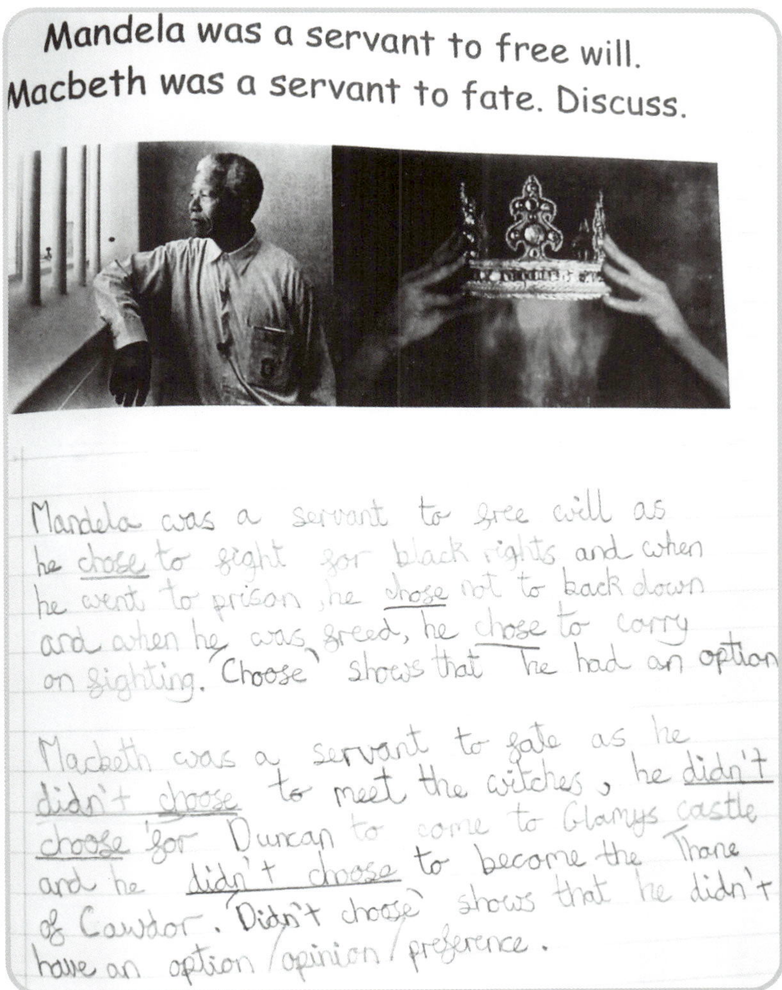

Mandela was a servant to free will.
Macbeth was a servant to fate. Discuss.

Mandela was a servant to free will as he chose to fight for black rights and when he went to prison, he chose not to back down and when he was freed, he chose to carry on fighting. 'Choose' shows that he had an option

Macbeth was a servant to fate as he didn't choose to meet the witches, he didn't choose for Duncan to come to Glamys castle and he didn't choose to become the Thane of Cawdor. 'Didn't choose' shows that he didn't have an option/opinion/preference.

Demonstrate understanding through applying what they have learned in their own writing

As a class, model how to write a short poem using the format and style of *Invictus* about Mandela's life. Children could then write their own short poem, in the same style, about Macbeth.

Our thanks to Lucy Aldridge and her Year 5 team at Warren Road Primary School for the planning and worked examples.